A SPORTING ALMANAC

RUGBY

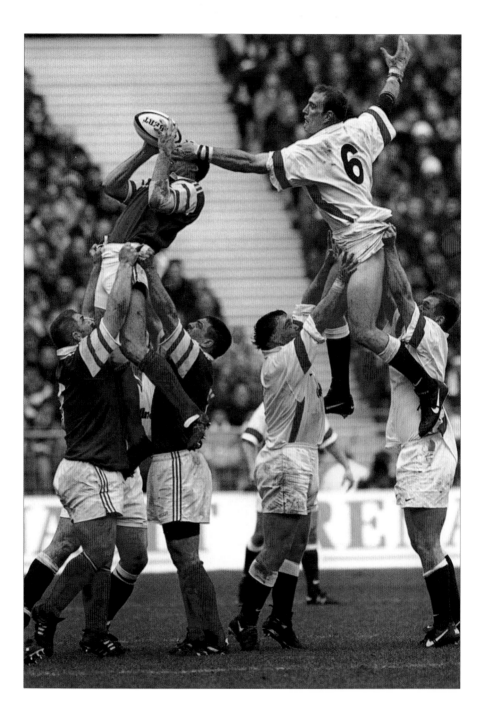

A SPORTING ALMANAC

RUGBY

Photographs by the
Daily Mail

Tim Hill

CONTENTS

THE ORIGINS OF THE GAME

Everyone knows the story. During a football match at Rugby School, William Webb Ellis suddenly decided to pick up the ball and run with it. And thus a new game was born.

Or was it? Ellis certainly was a 16-year-old student at Rugby School in 1823, the year in which this seismic sporting event was said to have taken place. Some 60 years elapsed until scholars of the game began to take an interest in its origin. Ellis himself was dead, the memories of those still alive inevitably hazy. Some of the early histories made no mention at all of Ellis, although naturally enough, Rugby School's own version of events trumpeted the part played by one of its sons in the beginnings of the game that bore its name. As far as that institution was concerned, the truth was set in stone - quite literally. A plaque at the school makes the claim boldly and unequivocally:

'This stone commemorates the exploits of William Webb Ellis who with a fine disregard for the rules of football as played in his time first took the ball in his arms and ran with it thus originating the distinctive feature of the rugby game - AD 1823.'

First official rules

There is a snag, however. In 1823 the laws of football were not codified, and all manner of rules existed in different parts of the country. These included handling the ball, which was the case at Rugby School, although running it with it was not allowed. In other words the situation was fluid; rules were made and changed on a whim.

In 1845 rugby's first official rules were drawn up, with the approval of the senior boys at Rugby School. The insistence on a clean catch was Rule No 1, and so the concept of the knock-on was there right from the start. The following year saw the publication of The Laws Of Football As Played At Rugby School. But this didn't represent any great innovation or departure from the games of football that were taking place up and down the country. Indeed, the game that was codified in these rules was broadly akin to the football that had been played for hundreds of years. The true radicals were those who only wanted to play the game with their feet. These dissenting voices included those at Cambridge and Eton, who objected to running with the ball and scrummaging, two of the features of modern rugby football. They also wanted to see an end to hacking - kicking an opponent's shins. Games of football involving dozens of players per side were invariably violent, and fatalities were not unknown. Usually players took the rough with the smooth and relished the battle. It was even said that the aggression that was central to the game helped to sustain Great Britain as an imperial power. But the risk of injury, which might render someone unable to work, could not be overlooked, and this was also a factor in the eventual schism.

The Cambridge Rules

On October 26 1863, representatives from twelve leading football clubs met at the Freemasons' Tavern, Great Queen Street, London to establish a clear set of laws for the game. A new body, the Football Association, was promptly formed. Reaching consensus on the rules proved to be trickier, and meetings were held over the next six weeks to thrash out the details. The new laws were broadly based on the Cambridge Rules, to the disappointment of the one lone voice, Blackheath FC. Blackheath fought hard to have some of the elements of the game as played at Rugby School adopted. When its representations fell on deaf ears, Blackheath resigned from the FA, allowing the club the freedom to continue playing the version of the game it favoured.

The Rugby Football Union

While Blackheath FC was holding out against the staunch advocates of Association Football, the old boys of Rugby School were also spreading the gospel. Old Rugbeians ventured forth into the universities and thence on to far-flung outposts of the empire, and the game went with them. Rugby football also made the short journey across the Channel and became popular in France.

In January 1871, some seven years after Association Football had brought standardisation to its game, rugby did the same. The Rugby Football Union had been formed the previous month and a number of clubs, including Blackheath, met to consider the rules under which all games should be played. They were broadly in line with those we recognise today but with some interesting exceptions. There were no points for a try. Touching the ball down over the opposition's line merely earned 'a try at goal'. It was the number of goals that decided the outcome, with tries counting only if the scores were level. Nor was the

A recent re-enactment of the famous occasion in 1823 when William Webb Ellis decided to pick up the ball and run with it. In 1839 Queen Adelaide, widow of William IV, visited Rugby School and watched a game on the famous sporting field. The boys had been given a tasselled cap to commemorate the visit, and some of them wore the headgear on the field of play. That didn't catch on, but the idea of presenting caps as a way of honouring international appearances did.

number of players laid down. When England and Scotland met in Edinburgh on 27 March 1871, it was a 20-a-side game. This historic encounter, the first rugby international, ended in a victory for Scotland, who scored a try and a goal to a solitary goal

Previous page: Some of the members of Richmond's first XV in 1877.

by England. Scotland's try which led to the winning goal was hotly disputed. Twenty years later the referee was still agonising as to whether he had made the correct decision.

That inaugural international match took place 48 years after William Webb Ellis supposedly showed 'a fine disregard for the rules of football'. It is almost certainly an apocryphal tale, but one which has become embedded in the folklore of the game. Does it matter? Surely not, for rugby, like all sport, is not just about players, rules and statistics. It is also about romance. The commemorative plaque at Rugby School bears testimony to the fact that rugby football had the most romantic of beginnings.

The Four Nations Championship

In the 1880s the game of rugby seemed to be in a healthy state. Ireland, Scotland and Wales had also formed their own Unions, and the 1882-83 season saw the Four Nations Championship contested for the first time. If anything, rugby was about to become a victim of its own success. Some thirty years after the meeting at the Freemasons' Tavern which precipitated the parting of the ways between rugby football and Association Football, the game was about to be split in two. It wasn't about rules this time; it was about money and livelihoods.

By the 1880s the tentacles of the game had stretched far beyond the playing fields of the public schools and the great universities. It was no longer the preserve of the professional classes, for whom sport was an entertaining diversion to be embraced and enjoyed whenever the opportunity presented itself. Rugby was now a mass participation sport. It was positively thriving in Lancashire and Yorkshire, where clubs such as Wigan, St. Helens, Leeds, Bradford and Hull drew sizeable crowds. As gate money increased, these clubs were keen to keep their own best players - and perhaps attract one or two from their rivals - by offering financial inducements. The structure of the game as then constituted did not allow for any payments, not even recompense for losses incurred by players having to take time off work.

Football had had the same arguments. In 1882 the Football Association relented over reimbursement of lost wages, hoping that would put an end to the growing resentment. It didn't. Professionalism was an open secret in football, and in 1885 the sport's governing body decided that pragmatism was the way forward and made legal what we would now call 'shamateurism'.

Inevitably, rugby was faced with the same dilemma. The RFU continued to bang the drum for the noble amateur. Far from shrugging their shoulders and saying 'if you can't beat 'em, join 'em', the game's administrators reaffirmed their vehement opposition to professionalism. Matters came to a head at a meeting of the RFU at the Westminster Palace Hotel, London, on 20 September 1893. Representatives from Northern clubs made their feelings plain by tabling a motion which would allow players to be paid for 'bona fide loss of time'. RFU officials must have had feelings of smug satisfaction when the result was declared. It was a decisive victory for the establishment and the status quo: 282 votes to 136. The RFU had made sure it had 120 proxy votes in the bag to help carry the day.

The Birth of Rugby League

But it was a hollow victory. Delegates from Halifax, Wakefield et al had no intention of returning home with their tails between their legs. If the RFU had hoped for passive acceptance, that august body was about to be sorely disappointed. Positions became even more entrenched. Secession was in the air. It eventually came two years later, 29 August, 1895. Representatives from 22 clubs across Yorkshire and Lancashire gathered at the George Hotel in Huddersfield and made the historic decision to break away from the RFU. 'Broken-time' payments would be perfectly acceptable in the Northern Rugby Football Union, as the new body would be called. 28 years later, in 1923, that name would be changed to Rugby League.

The birth of the professional era had a catastrophic effect on England's performances on the pitch. The northern clubs had been a breeding ground for the best players, and these were no longer available to the selectors. In the ten Home Nations championships that had been contested up to 1895, England had either won or shared top spot in five of them. After the schism of 1895, England went into a decline which was not halted until 1910, when Adrian Stoop led the side to the title.

W.W.Wakefield introduces the English team to King Edward VII before the Calcutta Cup in 1924. England and Scotland played their first rugby international in 1872 but the Calcutta cup was not at stake until 1878.

The Modern Era

The arguments that split rugby down the middle in the 1890s seem quaint in 2003. Rugby Union has now also embraced professionalism, although it took a hundred years to do so. The north-south divide has become blurred: Newcastle Falcons, boasting England's star half-back Jonny Wilkinson, flies the Union flag, while the Broncos have given Rugby League a foothold in the capital. A decade ago Bath, then top dogs in the 15-man game, met the all-conquering Wigan side in a fascinating cross-code clash, one which has been repeated since. A succession of players have shown that the skills are eminently transferable. Jonathan Davis, Henry Paul, Iestyn Harris and Jason Robinson are among those who have lit up both codes. Va'aiga Tuigamala starred for the All Blacks, was hugely successful at Wigan, then returned to Union with Newcastle. The trend for two-way traffic looks set to continue. There are those who look at all these factors and entertain the idea of taking the best from both games and reuniting them under the simple banner: Rugby.

Below: England's star half-back Jonny Wilkinson

MILESTONES

1823   William Webb Ellis is said to have picked up the ball and run with it, 'thus originating the distinctive feature of the rugby game'.

1843   Blackheath, rugby's oldest club, is formed.

1845   First set of rules drawn up at Rugby School

1851   A 'Rugby School football' - an oval-shaped ball inflated by a pig's bladder - is displayed at the Great Exhibition in London. It was made by William Gilbert.

1863   Blackheath withdraws from the Football Association.

1870   RFU founded.
Rugby introduced to New Zealand by Charles Munro. Munro, who played the game at school in Sherborne, Dorset, was instrumental in the formation of New Zealand's first club, Nelson.

1871   England and Scotland contest the first international match.
The Rugby Football Union is formed at a meeting at the Pall Mall Restaurant, London.

1872   France's first Rugby Club formed by British residents at Le Havre.
England beat Scotland in their first home International, staged at Kennington Oval.
Calcutta RFC formed.

1873   Formation of the Scottish Rugby Football Union.

1875   Rugby introduced to South Africa by British soldiers garrisoned there.
Ireland play their first match, losing to England at Kennington Oval.

1877   Teams in international matches reduced from 20 to 15 players. Five years later this was extended to matches at all levels.

1878   First Calcutta Cup match, played at Kennington Oval. It was a scoreless draw.

1879   Irish Rugby Union formed, ending a five-year rift between north and south during which time Ulster had its own governing body.

1880   Welsh Rugby Union formed.

1883   Seven-a-side rugby 'invented' by Melrose. Straitened financial circumstances forced the border club to adopt the abbreviated form of the game, which became an instant success.

1888   The first British touring team goes to Australia and New Zealand.

1890   International Board founded. England gets six seats, with two each for Wales Scotland and Ireland.

1890   Barbarians RFC founded.

1895   Rift over broken-time payments sees northern clubs break away to form their own league.

1906   France lose to New Zealand 38-8 in the country's first international match, staged at Parc des Princes.

1910   First international match at Twickenham. England beat Wales 11-6 and go on to win their first championship since the schism of 1895.
France enter the championship for the first time.

1922   In the Wales v England match at Cardiff both teams wear numbered shirts for the first time. Wales ran out 28-6 winners.

1924   Cyril Brownlie becomes the first international player to be sent off, in the All Blacks match against England.

1924   Murrayfield becomes the headquarters of Scottish rugby. The inaugural international is played there the following year.

Below: 1939: England, captained by H.B. Toft, are ready to face Ireland in the last Home International tournament before the outbreak of war. Ireland won 5-0.

1931 The Bledisloe Cup introduced for Australia v New Zealand matches. The four Home Unions break off relations with France over payments to players.

1938 England v Scotland at Twickenham becomes the first televised international match. Scotland win 21-16.

1939 France readmitted to the fold by the Home Unions, although outbreak of war means that no matches would be played until 1946-47.

1948 For financial reasons the touring Australian side asks for an extra fixture. They play Barbarians, on 31 Jan, the first time that the club had met a touring side.

1948 Points value of a dropped goal reduced from 4 to 3. Australia, New Zealand and South Africa admitted to the International Rugby Board.

1951 Lansdowne Road, Dublin, takes over from Ravenhill, Belfast as the headquarters of Irish rugby.

Below: 1978: The ball hangs in the air as England's Rafter finds himself surrounded by All Blacks who went on to win 16-6.

1967 New Zealand postpone a tour to South Africa over the refusal of the South African government to allow Maoris in the touring party.

1968 Replacements permitted in international matches.

1970 Players allowed to kick into touch on the full from inside their own 25-yard line.

1971 Points value for a try increased from 3 to 4.

1972 The championship not completed for the first time in 74 years, as Wales and Scotland refuse to play Ireland because of terrorist threats.

1973 The only quintuple tie ever in the championship, as all five nations win twice and lose twice.

1978 France becomes the eighth member of the International Rugby Board.

1979 Wales win the Triple Crown for a record fourth successive year.

1987 Inaugural World Cup staged in Australia and New Zealand.

1992 Points value for a try increased from 4 to 5.

2000 The first Six Nations Championship contested as Italy joins the annual international series.

CHANGES IN SCORING

No points were awarded for a try until 1887. Even then a touchdown was worth just one point, compared to 3 points for a goal. It wasn't until all four Home Nations became members of the International Rugby Board that a uniform system of scoring was adopted. The following table shows the amendments that have been made since then.

	TRY	CONVERSION	PENALTY GOAL	DROPPED GOAL	GOAL FROM MARK
1890	1	2	2	3	3
1891	2	3	3	4	4
1893	3	2	3	4	4
1905	3	2	3	4	3
1948	3	2	3	3	3
1971	4	2	3	3	3
1978	4	2	3	3	–
1992	5	2	3	3	–

Opposite: England captain Will Carling is tackled by Australia's Tim Horan in the 1991 World Cup final. Australia won 12 - 6, Daly and Lynagh scoring for Australia and Webb converted two penalties for England.

THE LIONS

T he British Lions owe a great debt to three cricketers who toured Australia in 1877. Messieurs Shaw, Shrewsbury and Stoddart had such a good time that they thought rugby ought to follow crickets' example. They approached the RFU, who had no objections as long as amateur status was not compromised. On 8 March 1888 a touring party left for Australia and New Zealand. Consisting mainly of Englishmen, together with a few

Scots and a lone Manxman, the tourists were away for nine months. They played 54 matches in total, some of them under Australian Rules. There were two defeats, both against New Zealand opposition.

It is generally accepted that the first side which was truly representative of the four home nations was that which toured South Africa in 1910, the Springboks winning the three-match series 2-1. The 'Lions' tag - after the logo on the team tie - was not applied to the Great Britain representative side until 1924, when South Africa was also the destination. The Springboks again prevailed, winning three of the four matches, with one game drawn.

The team pictured at the start of their tour of Australia in 1971.

THE BARBARIANS

he Six Nations Championship, Tri-Nations Series, World Cup; all prestigious events in the Rugby calendar. But players regard an invitation to turn out for the Barbarians as a unique honour.

The Barbarians Club was formed in 1890 after a home counties representative side had gone on tour and fulfilled a series of holiday fixtures over Christmas and Easter. The tour had been so successful and enjoyable that some of its members decided to form a club specifically to play end-of-season matches. Since then, all those invited to play naturally adhere to the Barbarians' principle of attacking, free-flowing rugby.

The tradition of the Barbarians taking on international touring sides dates back

to 1947-48, when the Wallabies wanted an extra match to boost their coffers. The Barbarians won that game 9-6 and it has been a fixture on the calendar ever since.

The Barbarians were involved in one of the most thrilling games ever seen, when they took on the All Blacks at Cardiff Arms Park on 21 January 1973. The Barbarians side consisted largely of the players who had gone on the famous 1971 Lions tour. One exception was Phil Bennett, who had replaced Barry John at fly-half following the 'King's' retirement. After barely two minutes, Bennett picked up the ball deep in defence and sidestepped his way past three opponents. It was the start of a stunning seven-man move which ended with Gareth Edwards diving over in the corner. Slattery, Bevan and JPR Williams also touched down for the Barbarians, while Grant Batty went over twice for New Zealand. The final score was 23-11 to the Barbarians, but that was of secondary importance to the regal show that had been put on by two star-studded teams.

Below: Gareth Edwards playing for the Barbarians against the All Blacks in 1967 passes the ball out before he is tackled by New Zealand's scrum half C.R. Laidlaw.

TWICKENHAM

Until 1909 England played their matches at various venues, the RFU having no fixed base. William Williams persuaded the sport's governing body to spend £5,572 12 shillings and sixpence on a ten-and-a-half-acre site at Twickenham, which had previously been used for agricultural purposes. Two years after that historic decision in 1907, Harlequins beat Richmond in the first club match to be played at the ground. Twickenham first played host to international rugby in January 1910, when England beat Wales 11-6.

The crowd invade the pitch at the England Wales international match at Twickenham in 1950.

HALL of FAME

PHIL BENNETT

Phil Bennett had the unenviable task of putting on the famous Wales No. 10 shirt worn with such distinction by Barry John. In fact, John's premature retirement finally pushed the international door wide open for Bennett. He was already a star at Llanelli and had been capped, playing in various positions in the backs. He had his critics in his early days, but after the 'King's' retirement in 1972, 23-year-old Bennett finally established himself in the Wales team and as an outstanding fly-half in his own right. Who can forget his contribution to arguably the most famous try ever scored, for the Barbarians in the 1973 match against the All Blacks? His three outrageous sidesteps inside his own 25 turned defence into pulsating attack, resulting in Gareth Edwards diving over in the corner.

Edwards was to enjoy a longer partnership with Bennett than he had with John in an international shirt, and came to regard him as the second world class fly-half he had played with. Bennett may have lacked John's gazelle-like grace, but he too had dazzling foot work. His right boot had both power and accuracy, and he was a better tackler than his predecessor.

Below: Bennett scores Wales's first try in the 1978 international against France at Cardiff Arms Park. Wales won the match and also achieved the Grand Slam that year.

Bennett was in top form on the 1974 Lions tour of South Africa. He scored 103 points, and his try in the second test was a remarkable solo effort. In 1977 he captained the Lions side that went to New Zealand and Fiji, becoming only the second Welshman to achieve that honour. He also captained Wales to two Triple Crown's and a Grand Slam. After retiring from international rugby in 1978 he continued to give outstanding service to Llanelli.

SERGE BLANCO

As JPR Williams' career was coming to an end, Serge Blanco was emerging as the man to take over as the foremost full-back in world rugby. He could be inconsistent, but French rugby in the 1980s was epitomised by Blanco surging forward on the counter-attack, linking up brilliantly with the outstanding three-quarters that the team boasted.

Venezuelan-born Blanco played his club rugby for Biarritz Olympique, and early in his career he also took the field as a winger. He came to prominence in the late 1970s, and was finally capped in 1980, in Pretoria against South Africa. He went on to play 85 times for his country, beating Mike Gibson's world record. In the inaugural World Cup of 1987 France's semi-final against Australia witnessed a classic

Opposite: Blanco training with the French team in March 1991.

Blanco performance. In the dying minutes he put his team under pressure with an unwise pass. The penalty was conceded and Michael Lynagh obliged. Blanco more than made up for the error deep into injury time, when the French swept forward and the ball passed through several pairs of hands before Blanco went over in the corner.

He played the game instinctively, with a spontaneity that delighted rugby fans everywhere. Despite his weakness for the odd cigarette, he was fit enough and quick enough to have played well beyond 1991 when, at 33, he announced his retirement. His 33 tries put him second in the all-time list behind David Campese.

DAVID CAMPESE

avid Campese had little time for dour battles in which the forwards slugged it out while the backs kicked their heels. He could only have played in a team committed to 15-man rugby, and a team with 'Campo' in it would have been mad to do otherwise. Effervescent, ebullient, a consummate crowd pleaser, Campese always preferred to take a risk in the name of entertainment than play safe and induce boredom.

He made his Wallabies debut as a 19-year-old on the 1982 tour of New Zealand. The hallmarks of his game were there for all to see, and over the next decade and 54 internationals he racked up a world record tally of tries with his devastating running. He played at full-back as well as on the wing, but his

Opposite: David Campese salutes the crowd after his farewell international played against the Barbarians at Twickenham in 1996.

philosophy remained the same irrespective of his position on the pitch. In the third test against the Lions in Sydney in 1989, this philosophy came at a cost. He tried to run the ball out of defence, gave a suicidal pass and Ieuan Evans pounced to score the decisive try. But for every critic Campo had a thousand adoring fans, and not only those just those with Wallabies affiliations. Campese was at his mercurial best in Australia's World Cup victory in 1991. He bowed out against Wales at Cardiff Arms Park the following year, running in a typically brilliant solo try to round off a glorious career.

KEN CATCHPOLE

I n the 1960s Ken Catchpole set the standards that all aspiring scrum-halves tried to emulate. He had incredible hand speed and was regarded as one of the quickest passers the game had ever seen. He was equally adept on either side and his delivery was helped by the fact that he was always beautifully balanced. He and Phil Hawthorne, his regular midfield partner in the Wallabies side, formed one of the best half-back parings in history. Between 1961 and 1968 Catchpole was capped 27 times, captaining the side on thirteen occasions. He and Hawthorne created the platform for Australia to achieve far greater success than the quality of the side as a whole merited. Catchpole had an excellent kicking game, was a stout defender and a shrewd tactician. When Wilson Whineray's all-conquering All Blacks of 1963-64 came up against Australia, they lost 20-5, Catchpole showing once again that at least at scrum-half the New Zealanders had to defer to the master.

Catchpole's brilliant career came to an abrupt end, also in a match against their great rivals. He was burrowing into a ruck, one leg trailing into the air. Colin Meads arrived and yanked the protruding limb to clear a path. Unfortunately, Catchpole's other leg was locked firmly among the mass of bodies. His groin was badly torn and he never fully recovered. Although the premature end to his career was a pure accident, the incident hardly endeared Meads to Australia's rugby fans, who idolized 'Catchy'. He left a great legacy, however. Players and coaches continued to marvel at his technique long after his playing days were over.

Opposite: Catchpole, always balanced and alert, ready to pass the ball in January 1967.

DANIE CRAVEN

I n South Africa the name Danie Craven is synonymous with rugby football. Soccer was an early passion on the farm in Orange Free State where Craven grew up. He was 13 before he was introduced to the oval ball, and soon made up for lost time. He was too slight to be a forward, his preferred choice, and almost became a scrum-half by default. He is credited with inventing the dive pass, although in fact he experimented with this delivery after hearing that another scrum-half had tried it. It certainly became a formidable weapon in his armoury, enabling him to get extra length and accuracy with his passing.

Craven was a surprise selection for the Springboks' 1931-32 tour of Great Britain. He hadn't even represented his provincial side, but A F Markotter, the coach at Stellenbosch University where Craven was a student, knew that he was ready for the national team. South Africa won all their test matches and 21-year-old Craven enhanced his reputation as a world-class scrum half.

Opposite: Craven executes his famous 'dive pass' which allowed him to generate extra length and accuracy in his passing.

In 1937 Craven was vice-captain when the Springboks went to New Zealand. They lost the first test 13-7, with Craven moved to stand-off to accommodate Pierre de Villiers at scrum-half. Craven returned to his favourite position for the next two tests. His outstanding performances helped South Africa to a 2-1 series victory. In the deciding match Craven's famed long passing created a beautiful try. He took possession from a scrum and waved his stand-off further and further infield. The All Blacks moved across to cover, and Craven slipped a short pass to the blindside wing, who had acres of space to set up the score.

Craven captained the side when the Lions came to South Africa in 1938. The Springboks won the series 2-1 and 27-year-old Craven announced his retirement. He went on to have a long and and illustrious career as an administrator.

GERALD DAVIES

erald Davies made his debut for Wales against Australia in December 1966, the game in which Barry John also made his first international appearance. He played at centre that day, and on eleven other occasions. But it was as a winger that he achieved legendary status. Fortune played a part in the transformation. During Wales' tour of Australia in 1969 the squad boasted three fit centres but only one winger. Davies volunteered to give it a go. He scored a try and relished the freedom out wide, which was compensation for seeing less of the ball. Centre was also fast becoming a powerhouse position, and Davies realised where his future lay. Small of stature but with electrifying pace and the slipperiness of an eel, Davies was a defender's nightmare. His trademark sidestep was so fluid and so late that opponents had little chance to react.

He went to South Africa with the Lions in 1968, where he played in the third test at Cape Town. Three years later, when the tourists went to New Zealand he was at his most devastating. Exams at Cambridge meant that he joined the tour late. His four tries against Hawke's Bay were all virtuoso efforts which even the most hardened Kiwi had to applaud. In 1974 and 1977 he put family commitments before touring and the Lions were denied his services. In 1978 he played his 46th and final game for Wales. Fittingly it ended where it began, against Australia. The venue was Sydney Cricket Ground, and among the crowd were many Kiwis. They had watched him in awed disbelief seven years earlier and had made the pilgrimage to see the last hurrah of a rugby great.

JONATHAN DAVIES

Following in the grand tradition of John and Bennett a decade earlier, Jonathan Davis lit up Welsh rugby in the 1980s. He had attended Gwendraeth Grammar School, whose old boys included John and the illustrious player-coach Carwyn James. Davies had everything. His running, passing and kicking were magnificent. He could score as well as create, with dazzling flashes of virtuoso skill. When he was in possession there was an air of expectancy among the crowd and concern among the opposition ranks. Davies' international career got off to a winning start with a victory over England at Cardiff in 1985. By the following year he was not only a key member of the Five Nations side but feted by rugby fans everywhere for his imperious skills. Wales won the Triple

Crown in 1988, but this was not the world beating side of the 1970s. The tour of New Zealand that same year was typical of the era. In the second test in Auckland Davies scored a length-of-the-field try which left even the home fans purring, but it was scant consolation for a 54-9 hammering.

Davies had known hard labour, working long hours cleaning bulldozers. He felt his talents were unappreciated and, more importantly, unrewarded. His disenchantment with Welsh rugby resulted in a move to Rugby League in 1989. Widnes paid a reputed world record £225,000 to get their man, and Davies effortlessly made the transition to become a star performer in the 13-man game.

GARETH EDWARDS

Gareth Edwards inherited Ken Catchpole's mantle as the world's pre-eminent scrum-half. He had great natural attributes for the position: speed, terrific upper body strength and the suppleness of a gymnast. What he lacked in those early days at Millfield was passing ability, a worrying handicap for a No 9. Barry John was certainly less than impressed when the two first met. But Edwards also had a fierce competitive edge and a dedicated approach when it came to practice. He worked tirelessly on his skills. When his opposite number in the New Zealand team, Chris Laidlaw, showed off his bullet-like spin pass, Edwards was soon seen on the training field trying to match him.

Edwards made his debut for Wales at 19, against France in the 1967 Five Nations championship. In February the following year he led the side against Scotland, becoming Wales' youngest ever captain. He was a fixture in the team until 1978, the match against France at Cardiff bringing down the curtain on an illustrious career. His 53 caps was a record that stood until 1981, when JPR Williams set a new mark. Edwards' appearances were consecutive, however, which remained a world record. He scored a record 20 tries for his country, helping the team to five Triple Crowns and three Grand Slams. Edwards was a vital member of the victorious Lions teams that went to New Zealand and South Africa in 1971 and 1974 respectively. He also dived over to score what many regard as the finest try of all time, for the Barbarians against the All Blacks in 1973.

Below: Edwards clears the ball in the final test between the British Lions and the Springboks in 1974.

MARK ELLA

Mark was the most gifted of the three Ella brothers who played for Australia in the 1980s. Students of the game argue as to whether Mark Ella or Barry John was the most majestic fly-half of the modern era. He caught the eye in the the Australian Schoolboy XV which proved invincible in 1977. He broke into the Wallabies side in the tour to Argentina in 1979, and soon became a fixture in the test team. He was appointed captain in 1982, when he was just 23. In 1984 he was at the height of his powers when Australia came to Britain and inflicted a whitewash on all four countries. Ella scored a try in each game, the only player ever to achieve that feat. Veteran coaches hung on the words of the 25-year-old when he expounded his views on the game during that series. He was a strong advocate of running rugby, and said his own secret was quick hands rather than feet. He had no great kicking game, but was not unduly worried as he thought tactical kicking was a blight on modern fly-half play. Ella believed that giving away possession was ridiculous; you had to have the ball in hand to score a try.

Shortly afterwards he announced his retirement. His frosty relationship with coach Alan Jones was said to be the main reason for his decision. In his 25 tests he had played rugby from the Gods. He eventually returned to the stage to play for his beloved club side, Randwick. At 30 he still had opponents drooling over his performances, and some said that even then he could have returned to the test arena and re-established himself as the world's number-one fly half.

Below: Mark Ella (right) and his brother Glen in 1977 when, along with along their brother Gary, they played in the Australian Schoolboys XV.

GRANT FOX

rant Fox's antipodean contemporary and great rival Michael Lynagh scored more points than he did, but the Australian's tally came from more matches. In terms of points-per-game Fox heads the all-time list. He became a fixture in the All Blacks side in the run-up to the inaugural World Cup in 1987, where he bagged 126 points in six games contributing hugely to the team's success in the tournament. In the same year he struck a world record 10 conversions in the team's 74-13 demolition of Fiji. It is easy to reduce Fox's game to that of a kicking machine. He was certainly that, but he had many more strings to his bow. He was not a twinkle-toed dazzler out of the Barry John mould, but he was utterly clinical, ruthlessly efficient. He was an expert at assessing situations and weighing the options. Invariably his decision-making was spot on.

Opposite: Fox converts a penalty for New Zealand against England in the opening match of the 1991 World Cup at Twickenham.

Grant Fox was the quickest international to reach 100 points, and 200. He then had Don Clarke's All Blacks record of 207 points in his sights, and that fell in only his twelfth outing. By 1993 he had trebled Clark's haul. He retired the following year, having secured his place among the most effective fly-halves the game had ever seen.

DAVE GALLAHER

ave Gallaher not only captained the first All Blacks side which toured Britain in 1905, he was also responsible for taking the game to a different level. He analysed matches in a way that hadn't been done before, keeping reams of statistics to show which phases and moves brought most success. He was also a great innovator. He employed a seven-man scrum in a 2-3-2 formation, with the spare forward, invariably Gallaher himself, used to feed the ball to the scrum-half. He studied the binding so closely that his forwards regularly came out on top against packs with an extra man. Planned moves with code words were used, and all players were expected to have a number of tricks up their sleeves. The team experimented with decoy runs and miss moves that seem normal fare now but were revolutionary at the time. They even varied stud length according to conditions. Nothing was left to chance.

Gallaher emphasised possession, quick accurate passing and good support play as the key to success. British teams at the time often buried the ball in rucks to slow the game down - which was permitted at the time - and struggled against a team that set up a new phase of play so quickly. Unsurprisingly, Gallaher's men carried all before them, losing only one game in the 35-match tour. They went down by a single try against Wales, when the team was tired and injury-hit. Gallaher retired at the end of the tour and became a selector. His team was called 'The Originals'. The term 'All Blacks' was also coined during the tour, although exactly when it was first used is uncertain.

MIKE GIBSON

f ever a player could have trumpeted his playing ability it was Ireland's Mike Gibson. He was a master in all aspects of the game: a fluid, elusive runner, brilliant passer, great tactical kicker and a fine tackler. His first taste of international rugby was for Cambridge University against the outstanding 1963-64 All Blacks. His opposite number that day was Earle Kirton, who went into the game as an easy way of boosting his own confidence, which was then at a low ebb. Kirton later recalled that he knew immediately he was watching the best fly-half of his generation in action. He was nearly right. Gibson made his debut for Ireland at Twickenham in February 1964, the 22-year-old orchestrating his team's first victory over England for 16 years. By the time Barry John was in his pomp, Gibson had moved to centre, and even played on the wing towards the end of his career. Some still maintain that he could have been the greatest fly-half of them all.

Gibson went on four Lions' tours. In 1971 John grabbed the headlines, but purists recognised the huge contribution Gibson made to the series victory. For a man of his supreme gifts Gibson was self-effacing to the point of diffidence. Some geniuses strut on stage, Gibson didn't. The curtain rang down in fine style, with shock back-to-back victories over the Wallabies in Australia in 1979. His 81 caps in a glorious 16-year career was a world best, eclipsing the record set by Willie John McBride. It stood for more than a decade, when Serge Blanco set a new mark.

The British Lions team before leaving for their tour of South Africa in 1968. Mike Gibson, is sitting far left on the front row.

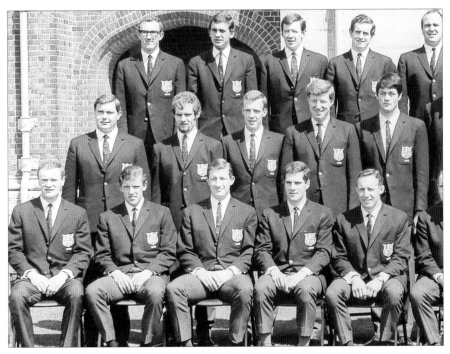

ANDY IRVINE

he voice of rugby, Bill McLaren, once said that along with David Campese, Andy Irvine was the player who gave him most pleasure. High praise indeed from a man who had been an avid spectator and commentator for some 60 years. Like Campo, Irvine played the game with exuberance and spontaneity. He too was an adventurous risk-taker, and when he was in possession a buzz of anticipation went round the ground.

Edinburgh-born Irvine made his international debut against New Zealand at Murrayfield in December 1972. The 21 year-old was on the receiving end of a 14-9 defeat that day. By the time he bowed out against Australia a decade later he had won a record 51 caps for Scotland, fifteen of them as captain. There were just 19 victories, but Irvine's individual prowess went far beyond the success of the team. He was often compared to his contemporary JPR Williams. The Welsh legend was considered better

defensively, Irvine having the edge as an attacking force. Selectors experimented by playing him on the wing, but eventually decided that Irvine was at his most potent bursting through from deep positions. Opponents became so wary of his forward forays that the cover they deployed often helped create space for Irvine's teammates.

Irvine was the first player to amass 300 points in international rugby. He made nine appearances for the Lions on the tours of 1974, 1977 and 1980, starring in the trip to New Zealand in '77. He ran in five tries against Taumarunui, a world record for a full-back. Irvine was awarded the MBE for his services to the game.

BARRY JOHN

nown simply as 'The King', Barry John's reign as the world's best fly-half was all too short. His decision to retire at the end of the 1971-72 season, at the age of 27, stunned Welsh rugby. But in the six years in which he graced the international stage, John left the fans with countless moments of genius to savour.

In Cefneithin, where John was born, mining was the lifeblood, rugby the grand passion. In his early days he played a lot of football, honing the skills which would serve him well on the rugby field. He would go to Stradey Park to watch Carwyn James in action. John followed in James' footsteps, both for Llanelli and Wales. In 1966, 21-year-old John was praised for his performance against the touring Australians. In December of that year he was awarded his first cap against same opposition. Wales lost the match, but John again excelled. Wales experimented with several half-back pairings over the following months. It was at the beginning of the 1967-68 season that the selectors paired John with Gareth Edwards. Over the next five years the two proved themselves to be among the greatest midfield partnerships of all time. Both were selected for the 1968 Lions trip to South Africa, but it wasn't a happy experience for John, whose tour was ended by a broken collarbone in the first test.

Opposite: Barry John outruns the England defence at Twickenham in February 1970.

1971 saw John at the height of his powers. His precision kicking and wraith-like running helped Wales to the Grand Slam. He then went to New Zealand again, and in only the 8th game of the tour he passed the 100-point tally set by South Africa's Gerry Brand in 1937, a record thought to be unassailable. By the end of the tour he had racked up 180 points and played a pivotal role in the historic 2-1 test series victory. John was again outstanding in the 1971-72 Five Nations championship, scoring a record 35 points as Wales retained their title. Soon afterwards the announcement came that the king was abdicating.

JACK KYLE

ohn Wilson Kyle first played for Ireland in 1946, in one of the 'Victory' series of Internationals that were staged before the championship proper resumed following the Second World War. The 19-year-old had excelled for Ulster School XV and the selectors had great hopes for their young star fly-half as he turned out against England at Lansdowne Road. Jack didn't disappoint. Ireland won that game and went on to achieve back-to-back Triple Crowns in 1947 and 1948. Kyle was the architect behind the most successful period in Ireland's history. He cut a slight figure on the pitch and sometimes appeared languid to the point of indolence. But he had the uncanny knack of being able to explode into life when the opportunity presented itself and when the opposition least expected it. Cliff Morgan found that to his cost when, as a nervous rookie, he faced the legendary Kyle in March 1951.

Opposite: Kyle at the height of his career in 1952.

Kyle won 47 caps for Ireland in his eleven years on the international stage, a fly-half record unsurpassed until Rob Andrew set a new mark in the 1990s. He toured New Zealand with the Lions in 1950, scoring a wonderful try in the first test at Dunedin. That game ended 9-9, and although the All Blacks won the next three tests, the series was won and lost in the forwards; Kyle and the rest of the backs were more than a match for the New Zealanders. Kyle ended his international career with a victory over Scotland in 1958. He carried on for a time with his club side NIFC before hanging up his boots to concentrate on medicine.

JONAH LOMU

he memory of Jonah Lomu's four-try demolition of England in the semi-final of the 1995 World Cup will live long in the memory. Although the All Blacks lost to hosts South Africa in the final, nothing could detract from the impact Lomu made. While he was being named Player of the Tournament, Will Carling and others were left scratching their heads about how to deal with such a phenomenon.

The statistics are revealing: 6 ft 5 in, 19 stone, size 13 boots and a best time of 10.8 seconds for the 100 metres. Lomu has the build of a mountainous forward, and in his schooldays he played at lock, flanker and No 8.

It was at the Hong Kong Sevens in 1994 that this unique combination of power and pace was brought to the attention of the wider public. He made his All Blacks debut the same year against France. At 19 years 45 days he became New Zealand's youngest ever test player. He suffered a series of nagging injuries and was also diagnosed as suffering from a rare kidney disease. Treatment for that condition has meant long periods on the sidelines. That hasn't stopped representatives from Rugby League and American football from attempting to woo him away from the code in which he has become a megastar. Lomu shows no signs of relinquishing his No. 11 All Blacks jersey, and at 28 he still has a long future as the most potent gamebreaker and try scorer in world rugby.

MICHAEL LYNAGH

Michael Lynagh was a golden-haired golden boy of Australian sport in the early 1980s. A low handicap golfer and an international cricketing prospect, Lynagh delighted Australia's selectors when he opted to concentrate on rugby. After turning out for the country's Schoolboys XV, Queensland University and the Queensland state side, it was a question of when he would be awarded his first full cap. He made a solid debut against Fiji in 1984, then made his mark in the Grand Slam-winning tour of Britain. Lynagh played centre, the mercurial Mark Ella occupying fly-half berth. Victories over England, Ireland and Wales left Australia needing a win at Murrayfield to complete the clean sweep. Lynagh had been struggling with his kicking, but popped over 15 out of 16 in solitary practice on the eve of the match, and was back on song in the 37-12 victory.

Ella's retirement left Lynagh in possession of the No. 10 shirt. Coach Bob Dwyer believed there was nothing to choose between the two. Ella may have had more magic, but Lynagh's kicking was superior. Lynagh overhauled Hugo Porta's world record 564 points in 1990, and by the time he retired five years later he had accumulated 911 points from his 72 international appearances. He scored a sensational late try against Ireland in the quarter-final of the 1991 World Cup, when the favourites looked in danger of going out. After beating holders New Zealand in the semis, Australia won the tournament with a 12-6 win over England, Lynagh scoring eight points. He bowed out after the quarter-final defeat by England in the 1995 tournament. It was his despairing dive which just failed to charge down Rob Andrew's famous drop goal which sealed victory for England.

JO MASO

France's current team manager Jo Maso was the star of the side in the late 1960s and early 1970s. He is widely regarded as the best of the long line of magical three-quarters that France has produced of the years. In the 1990s he was inducted into the hall of fame in one of the game's popular periodicals. And yet Maso's prodigious skills and inventiveness were not fully appreciated by the selectors at the time. He was discarded in 1973, when he was just 28. France enjoyed considerable success in the seven years that Maso performed on the international stage. They won the Five Nations in 1967 and 1968, and took a

share of the championship in 1970 and 1973. But there was a fallow period in which France failed to register a win in ten matches. Whether Maso, with his extravagant individual skills, was deliberately made a scapegoat for this poor run is unclear. But he found himself unsure of his place in the team. If the selectors had their doubts, they weren't shared by the fans, who were quick to pay homage to a player whose flair epitomised the very best in French rugby. Maso continued to shine for his club side, Narbonne, after finding himself in the International wilderness. Most aficianados agree that this gem of a player's rightful place was at the game's top table, and that the 25 caps with which he ended his career was a poor return for the gifts he possessed.

WILLIE JOHN MCBRIDE

long with his contemporary Colin Meads, Willie John McBride inspired a generation of forwards. He won 63 caps for Ireland and made 17 appearances for the Lions over a remarkable five tours. His 80 caps was a record until his fellow-countryman Mike Gibson went one better in 1979.

1962 saw 21-year-old McBride make his first appearance for Ireland and for the Lions, who went to South Africa. He finished on the losing side in the two tests he played in. Things got worse before they got better. The All Blacks won all four games when the Lions went to the antipodes in 1966, the first ever whitewash in a four-match series. The All Blacks' forwards were dominant throughout. There was further disappointment in South Africa in 1968, but in 1971 it all came right. McBride was part of a pack which could now hold its own against the All Blacks, creating a platform for the team's excellent attacking players. Even Meads, MacBride's great rival, had to accept that the better team won the series. In 1974 McBride captained the side in what was his third trip to South Africa. He led the team to a famous series victory, one dominated by the forwards. Some regarded the performances as uninspiring. It was also quite brutal. This was the series of the famous '99' call, when McBride's men waded into the opposition when the signal was given. McBride believed that the Lions had come off worst in the physical encounters in the past and was determined it should not happen again. For him the end justified the means, and it meant that he finally tasted success against the Springboks. 1974 also saw McBride captain Ireland to the Five Nations championship, the country's first success since 1951. He retired the following year, acclaimed and respected for his contribution to the game.

Opposite: McBride jumps in the line-out when Ireland faced England in the 1974 home international tournament. This was McBride's 56th appearance for Ireland.

COLIN MEADS

olin Meads was a towering presence in the All Blacks team which dominated world rugby in the 1960s. Meads, who was given the nickname Pine Tree, was a fringe player during the stormy test series between the New Zealand and South Africa in 1956. The All Blacks had an ageing pack and there was concern as to whether forwards of the required calibre would come through to replace them. Enter Colin Meads. He made his debut in 1957, and although he often played at loose forward, he soon made the position of lock his own. He was a fearless and fearsome competitor. In the early days he was the arch exponent of the All Blacks' uncompromising forward play around which the team built its success . No quarter was asked - or given. On the 1966 Lions' tour of New Zealand he knocked out David Watkins, and in 1969 he broke Welsh hooker Jeff Young's jaw. Australia's scrum half Ken Catchpole's career was ended by a groin injury sustained when Meads all but ripped his leg out of its socket. On the famous 1967 tour of Britain Meads was sent off against Scotland for a lunging kick at fly-half David Chisholm as the latter was about to gather the ball. Such incidents were more to do with total commitment than violent conduct, and Meads' opponents had nothing but the utmost respect for him. His career ended on a low note, captaining the All Blacks side which lost to the Lions in 1971. But in his record 55 tests the man who reportedly trained by running up hills with a sheep under each arm had done more than enough to secure a place in rugby's hall of fame.

CLIFF MORGAN

n 1951 Cliff Morgan emerged from Wales' fly-half production line and held sway for the next seven years. Morgan had been soccer mad as a schoolboy, as so many great number tens were. His conversion came at Tonyrefail Grammar School, where he was influenced by a craft teacher who was a rugby fanatic. He went through the local ranks and then eventually made it into the Cardiff side. Then, in March 1951, he made a nervous international debut at the Arms Park. Ireland provided the opposition, and Morgan found himself up

against one of his heroes, Jack Kyle. Kyle seemed to be having an off-day, and Morgan momentarily lost concentration. The legendary Irish fly-half scored, and Morgan never forgot the lesson.

Later the same year Morgan blamed himself for Wales' defeat by South Africa, when the Springbok flanker Basie van Wyk pressurised him into too much aimless kicking. Four years later Morgan was a more mature, more complete performer and he had his revenge against the same player. He starred for the Lions during that 1955 tour of South Africa, scoring a breathtaking solo try in the first test at Ellis Park. The Lions won 23-22. Morgan took over the captaincy for the third test, which the Lions also won. The series finished 2-2, and Morgan won over the partisan crowds with his sparkling attacking play. He was a key member of Wales' Grand Slam-winning side of 1952, and captained his country to the championship in 1956. His golden moment for Cardiff came in 1953, when he helped the team to a historic 8-3 victory over the All Blacks.

GRAHAM MOURIE

raham Mourie captained the All Blacks in 19 test matches between 1977 and 1982. In that time he established himself both as a great player and leader, following in the tradition of such luminaries as Wilson Whineray and Brian Lochore. Mourie was a superb back row forward, powerful and mobile, flint-hard and ultra-competitive. He was out of the same mould as his counterpart in France's side, Jean-Pierre Rives, and the two had the utmost respect for each other. Mourie's first full game as captain was in France, against a powerful representative side at Brive in 1977. He had already skippered the team against Argentina, but this game marked his real baptism. The All Blacks ran out 45-3 winners, and won much praise for the stylish play which would be a hallmark of the Mourie years.

Opposite: Mourie drives over the line, evading the Welsh scrum-half Terry Holmes. New Zealand won the match 23-3.

Mourie was a deep thinker. He saw the game as a cerebral as well as a physical battle. Those who played under him acknowledged his ability to read the game and make tactical decisions which invariably bore fruit. He was a great motivator, always able to get the best out of those around him while being a model of consistency himself.

It was not a period of unbroken success. The famous 1978 defeat by Munster sent shock waves through the camp. But this merely brought out another of Mourie's qualities, his marvellous sportsmanship. He also showed great character when, on moral grounds, he announced he was unavailable for the Springboks' tour of New Zealand. It was an unprecedented step for an All Blacks captain, but typical of the man.

GEORGE NEPIA

eorge Nepia was just 19 years old when he embarked on the 1924-25 All Blacks tour of Britain, France and British Columbia. Despite his youth, the Maori full-back proved to be the star of the 'Invincibles' side. He played in all 28 games, in which the team were unbeaten, thus going one better than their 1905 counterparts. The All Blacks persisted with the seven-man scrum, so their opponents had their share of possession. But if they got anywhere near the try line they invariably found Nepia performing heroics in defence. His positional sense was acute and his tackling formidable. Not for nothing was he likened to the Rock of Gibraltar.

Nepia didn't have a weakness. His catching, kicking and passing were flawless, and he was equally strong off either hand and both feet. He worked hard to hone his natural talents. He would lay down his blazer and practise dropping the ball onto it from the boot.

His game was built around stalwart defence, but he was no slouch when it came to joining the three-quarters and making the extra man in attack. In 1928 the All Blacks toured South Africa for the first time. Nepia should have starred on the country's fast grounds, but he was omitted from the squad because of the segregation laws that were in force. Without him, the All Blacks shared the series. Nepia returned the following year, showing he had lost none of his magic when the All Blacks went to Australia. Over 50 years later, in 1981, Nepia was at the forefront of the protest surrounding the Springboks' tour of New Zealand.

BENNIE OSLER

controversial but highly effective stand-off in the great Springboks side of the 1920s and early 1930s, Bennie Osler is 'credited' with the introduction of 10-man rugby. His kicking game was such a formidable tactical weapon that opposition sides constantly found themselves on the back foot. The South African forwards at the time were extremely powerful, winning a lot of possession and feeding the man with the magical boot. Osler guaranteed them

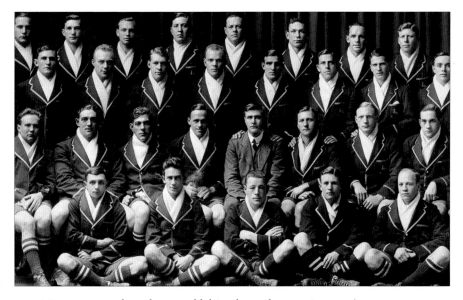

Above: The South African Springboks, pictured in 1924.

gaining more yardage than would have been the case in a running game. Once the ball was near the opposition's line the pressure built up and invariably resulted in a score, be it an Osler penalty or drop goal, and even the odd try. It wasn't pretty, and the three-quarters spend a lot of their time kicking their heels. But it was highly effective. When the All Blacks came up against Osler in 1928 they had no answer. Two drop goals - then worth four points each - and two penalties gave Osler 14 points in a 17-0 win.

Osler captained the side which toured England in 1931-32. He was critical of his own performances, but his kicking still had a major influence and South Africa enjoyed a clean sweep of the four international matches. The team lost just one game, against a Midland Counties XV. Osler didn't play and the Springboks came unstuck playing a more expansive game. In 1933, when South Africa met Australia, Osler played his usual game in the first test and the 'Boks ran out 17-3 winners. Stung by the constant criticism, Osler didn't kick at all in the next encounter. Australia won 21-6! Needless to say, he returned to his tried and trusted method thereafter, and South Africa took the series 3-2.

Osler played to his and the team's strengths. He played at a time when victory was more important than style, and he certainly influenced a generation of fly-halves.

HUGO PORTA

ugo Porta's sparkling international career lasted for almost two decades, putting him at the very pinnacle if one were to combine class with longevity. He would be very close to the top on quality alone. Graham Mourie, the All Blacks captain of the 1970s, and Michael Lynagh, who eventually overhauled Porta's record points haul, certainly thought so. Porta was not just a world class rugby player but a brilliant all round sportsman. He played soccer as a youngster and could well have taken it up professionally. He thus developed marvellous ball skills, and when he turned his attention from the round to the oval variety he was always its master, never its victim. Porta had the knack of looking uninterested, then exploding into life and wreaking havoc on opposition defences. He used clever changes of pace and direction rather than electrifying bursts to escape the clutches of opponents. He was an intuitive player, and kicked like a dream off both feet. More than one flanker who tried to contain Porta likened him to a matador, delaying his pass or movement until the last possible moment before executing the manoeuvre to perfection.

Right: Porta trains with the Argentinian Pumas at Bisham Abbey sports centre prior to their tour of England in 1978.

In 1974 Porta scored a world record seven penalties against France. Some 15 years later, nearing the age of 40 and with well over 500 points to his name, Porta was still in demand as the Pumas' playmaker and No 1 superstar.

JEAN-PIERRE RIVES

Jean-Pierre Rives once played against Australia with only one functioning arm. The other had been badly dislocated a couple of weeks earlier, but when an injury-hit side needed him, Rives didn't shirk the 'call to arms'. He took the field, to the amazement of both teammates and the Australians, and played as combatively as he could with one limb hanging limply. France lost the game, but Rives enhanced his reputation as a totally fearless, totally committed flanker.

Rives was born in Toulouse on 31 December 1952. He played club rugby for Toulouse and Racing Club. Rives made his first appearance for the national team as a 22-year-old against England at Twickenham on 1 February 1975. France won 27-20, and Rives embarked on an international career that would earn him 59 caps over nine years. It made him France's most capped flanker, and put him fourth in the country's all-time list.

In the early part of his career he played alongside two other great loose forwards, Jean-Pierre Bastiat and Jean-Claude Skrela. Rives took over the captaincy

from Bastiat in the 1978-79 season, and went on to lead the team on 34 occasions, a world record. France won 39, drew 3 and lost 17 matches during the Rives era. The highlights were undoubtedly 1977 and 1981, when France won the Grand slam for only the second and third time in history. No one contributed more than Rives. With his shock of blond hair he was easy to spot - and that was usually in the thick of the action. When the boots were flying and players had to put their bodies on the line, Rives was always there. Bloody head wounds seemed to be the norm. He went on to enjoy success as an actor and sculptor, but remains a hero to French rugby fans - their very own 'JPR'.

ADRIAN STOOP

drian Stoop was an outstanding fly-half for Oxford, Harlequins and England in the early years of the 20th century. But more than that he was a master strategist and innovator whose influence on the game reverberated into the modern era. When Stoop first played the game, fittingly at Rugby School, the half-backs regularly alternated positions. Stoop saw that specialisation was the way forward and he himself concentrated on the role of stand-off. He first played for England in March 1905, showing promise in a defeat by Scotland. He wasn't picked for the game against Dave Gallaher's All Blacks side nine months later, but the way the New Zealanders played undoubtedly had a deep effect on him. Like Gallaher, he took a scientific approach to the game. He too introduced code words for set plays, and was particularly interested in the importance of angles of running.

Stoop returned to international rugby in 1906, helping England to score wins over Scotland and France. Injury and bar examinations sidelined him for the best part of two seasons, but a poor run of results led to his recall as captain in 1910. His comeback was against Wales at the new Twickenham stadium. He collected the ball from the Welsh kick-off, and with some deft running and kicking he set up the ground's first ever try for winger F. Chapman. England ran out 11-6 winners, their first victory against Wales in over a decade. It also set the team on the road to a first championship since the schism with the Northern clubs in the 1890s. Stoop won fifteen caps, playing his last match in March 1912. Unlike many of his contemporaries, he played in a style much more akin to the modern fly-half.

WILLIAM WAVELL WAKEFIELD

ne of the game's great innovators and deep thinkers, William Wavell Wakefield set new standards for forwards in English rugby in the 1920s. Wakefield was powerfully built and a superb athlete. As a youth he worked on his tackling by taking flying leaps at pigs, a practice he heartily recommended. He also had an astute tactical brain, which he put to good effect in organising the forwards for Harlequins, Middlesex and England. Wakefield saw that specialised positional play could reap great dividends. He was a staunch advocate of wheeling the scrum to disrupt the opposition's defence at a time when such a tactic was hardly ever seen in top-class rugby. He also argued against the common practice of the scrum-half throwing in at the line-out. Wakefield saw that the scrum-half should be positioned ready to receive the ball or to cover if the opposition broke through. His idea soon became the norm.

Wakefield was captain of England when the 1924-25 All Blacks came to Britain. England started well against the the team dubbed 'The Invincibles'. They scored a try by Wakefield's favourite trick of wheeling the scrum near the All Blacks' line. They were about to repeat the move when a flare-up between the forwards resulted in the All Blacks' Cyril Brownlie being sent off. Wakefield maintained that the dismissal helped the opposition more than his side and New Zealand went on to win the match and maintain their 100% record.

Wakefield was capped 31 times between 1920 and 1927. His record for a back row forward stood for 40 years, when Budge Rogers set a new record.

J P R WILLIAMS

I n his youth JPR Williams was probably a better tennis player than rugby full-back. The junior Wimbledon champion was not a great kicker, which was then such an important weapon in the full-backs armory. But he was a model of reliability and consistency; he also tackled like an express train and was totally fearless. At no time was this better shown than in a match for his club side, Bridgend, against the All Blacks. A stamping incident left him with horrific facial injuries, yet he insisted on being patched up so that he could return to the fray.

He made his international debut against Argentina in 1968, when the JPR tag was soon applied to distinguish him from another John Williams, 'JJ'. He enhanced his reputation when Wales toured New Zealand in 1969, but it was the following year that he established himself as a world class full-back. The laws were amended so that players could no longer put the ball into

Williams trains at Eastbourne with the British Lions before setting off for thei 1971 tour of Australia and New Zealand.

touch on on the full from any part of the field. Williams used this to add a brilliant attacking dimension to his game. Over the next decade, one of the the hallmarks of JPR's play was rampaging forward runs.

Williams was a key member of the famous Lions teams of 1971 and 1974. In the fourth test against New Zealand at Eden Park, his monster drop goal helped the team to draw the match and thus confirm the 2-1 series victory. Williams' career spanned the golden era for Welsh rugby. The team won or shared eight Five Nations championships before he finally hung up his boots in 1981.

JONNY WILKINSON

Jonny Wilkinson has been such a vital cog in the England team for so long that it is hard to remember he is still only 24. With well over 500 points already to his name, only injury can prevent him streaking ahead and out of sight in the list of all-time top scorers.

Wilkinson was rugby mad even as a toddler, and although he was an excellent all-round sportsman, there was never any doubt in which field he would specialise. He appeared at Twickenham at the age of 10, playing for Farnham Boys in a cup-final curtain-raiser. He went on to play for England Schoolboys and was singled out as a future star. He has always been a perfectionist, and the combination of long hours on the training field and great natural ability have given Wilkinson a stature in the game to rival any of the Southern Hemisphere's big names. In 1987 he deferred going to Durham University to join Newcastle Falcons. There he became a protege to Rob Andrew, who moved to centre to accommodate the young prodigy. The former England star remarked that Wilkinson managed the step up in class to international rugby with ease, something that took him years.

Wilkinson made his England debut against Ireland in April 1998, becoming the country's youngest international for more than 70 years. He played at centre in the early days, including the 'tour of hell' down under, when England lost 76-0 to Australia. Mentally tough as well as supremely confident, Wilkinson had a spell out of the side, then returned an even stronger player. Clive Woodward moved him to fly-half, and he has been the lynchpin of the side ever since.

COMPETITIONS

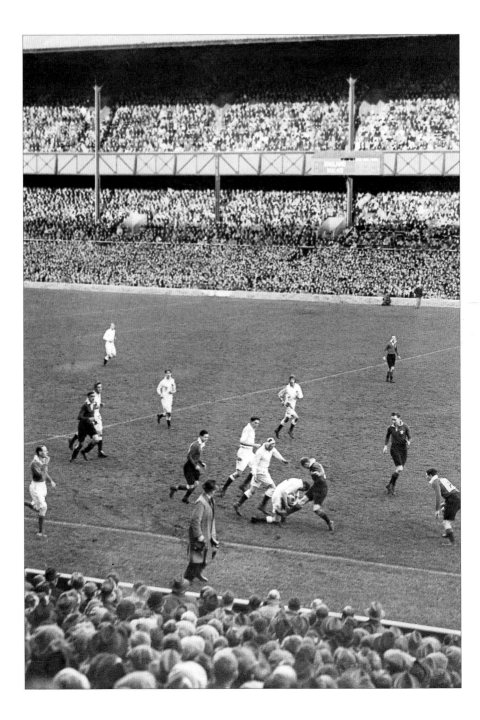

THE INTERNATIONAL CHAMPIONSHIP

he annual international competition involving the four home nations, France and, since 2000, Italy, had hazy beginnings. It started out as simply an annual series of fixtures between England, Scotland, Ireland and Wales. There was no trophy for the winner and it wasn't until the early 1890s - a decade after the series got under way-that the term 'championship' was applied to the round-robin event.

Early controversy

England and Scotland dominated the early years, winning between them the first nine completed championships. Two of England's successes, in 1884 and 1892, were a clean sweep of victories, the mythical Triple Crown. The first of those left a very sour taste in the mouths of the Scots. One of their players fisted the ball in a lineout - knocking back, as it was called. The English players appealed for an infringement and the Scots paused momentarily to await the referee's decision. Their opponents played on and scored the decisive try. Scotland refused to play England the following year as a result, and the rift was only healed when England agreed to join the International Rugby Board.

Scotland enjoyed great success in the 1880s by fielding three three-quarters instead of the usual two. After three championship victories, two of them shared, the Scots won their first Triple Crown in 1891.

System changes

Wales broke the stranglehold in the 1892-93 season. They did it in style, extending the Scots' idea regarding three- quarter play. Eager to play an expansive game even then, the Welsh played a revolutionary four three-quarter system, giving the team seven backs when most other sides fielded only six. Their rivals were initially sceptical, but such was the impact of the Welsh team that soon all the home nations were playing with two wingers and two centres.

The Irish had an indifferent start in their international matches. Matters weren't helped by an acrimonious internal row between North and South, following the formation of the Irish Rugby Union in Dublin in 1874. In 1882, when Ireland met Wales for the first time, in Dublin, two of their players

Opposite: A Welsh player stops an English rush during the first international of the 1937-8 season watched by 70,000 people at Twickenham.

were so incensed by the ferocity of the match that they walked off the pitch. Needless to say, Wales won. The ill feeling meant that there was no corresponding fixture the following year. When the two sides met in Cardiff in 1884, two of Ireland's players failed to turn upand emergency replacements had to be found - from the Welsh ranks! Wales prevailed again.

Ireland's first victory against England

In 1887, at the twelfth time of asking, Ireland finally notched their first victory against England. One of their players, John McCauley, had had all his leave entitlement so he used the loophole of getting married in order to get the time off. Ireland won by two goals to nil. This was the launchpad to a highly successful 1890s, in which Ireland won the championship three times, including the Triple Crown in 1894 and 1899. It would be nearly half a century before they would repeat that feat. Wales dominated the early years of the 20th century. They won the championship outright on six occasions, and shared the title with Ireland in 1905-06. The team suffered just seven defeats in 43 matches between 1900 and 1911, and were very good value for the six Triple Crowns gained during that period.

Below: Lowe scores one of England's tries in the Calcutta Cup of 1922. Forty thousand spectators at Twickenham watched England win 11 - 5.

Scotland also had their moments with four more championships, including the Triple Crown in 1901 and 1903. The team that was struggling was England, still reeling from the split over professionalism in the 1890s. Adrian Stoop was the inspiration behind the team which stopped the rot, in 1910. It was Stoop's mazy run which set up the score that helped England to an 11-6 victory over a shell-shocked Welsh side, who were then both champions and Triple Crown holders.

Above: In the early 1920s England dominated the competition led by William Wavell Wakefield (middle row, second from left). But this 1922 team were sensationally defeated 28-6 by Wales who went on to win the championship that year.

France join the championship

1910 was the first season in which Twickenham was used as an international venue. It also saw France join the championship. The French had been unperturbed by a string of early reverses on the international stage. Between 1906 and 1914 France lost 27 of the 28 games they contested. The chink of light came in 1911, when Scotland were beaten 16-15 at Stade Colombres. The floodgates didn't exactly open, however, and after that victory there were seventeen consecutive defeats up to 1920.

England lost 26 international players in World War One, including the

outstanding three-quarter Ronald Poulton. However, a host of new faces ushered in a golden era. England shared the championship with Scotland and Wales in 1920, then won it outright in three of the next four seasons. The forwards, led by

Above: France v. England in the Five Nations tournament in Paris in 1927. France won 3-0.

William Wavell Wakefield, were totally dominant in this period. In 1924 he led the side to their first victory over Wales in Swansea since 1895, and the team went on to complete the Grand Slam. Another clean sweep in 1928 meant that England had won four Grand Slams in eight years, six overall. At that time the other four countries had managed that achievement just twice between them, Wales in 1911 and Scotland in 1925. Die-hard Welsh fans insist that Wales completed the Grand Slam in 1908 and 1909 too, recording victories over France in the two years before the French officially joined the championship.

Scotland's success in 1925 was a dramatic one. They met England on 21 March at the new Murrayfield stadium, both teams having won their three matches. In an exciting encounter of fluctuating fortunes, Scotland's fly-half Herbert Waddell won the match with a late drop goal to give Scotland the championship, the Triple Crown, Grand Slam and Calcutta Cup. It was a wonderful inaugural international for the stadium and a rare treat for the 70,000-strong crowd.

Ireland also boasted a fine side in the mid-1920s. They went down just 6-0 to the 'Invincibles', the touring All Blacks of 1924-25, and the following year beat England, Scotland and France, only to have their Grand Slam hopes ended by Wales, who beat them 11-8 in Swansea. Ireland had the consolation of sharing the championship with Scotland, and the same countries repeated that the achievement in 1927.

Four Nations again

The 1930s saw a return to a Four Nations championship as France was ostracised over yet another row over professionalism. The French had made steady progress. They enjoyed their first victory on foreign soil in 1920, scoring five tries in a 15-7 win in Dublin. At Twickenham in 1922 it was England who needed a late score to salvage an 11-11 draw. France had had eleven

Below: Although football was always the majority sport, international rugby matches always attracted large attendances. So great was the pressure at the 1930 Wales v England match that a section of the crowd encroached on the pitch; Ambulance men had to give first aid.

straight defeats against England before then, and lost the next four too. They finally gained their first victory over the English in Paris in 1927, and took the same scalp in 1931. These were excellent sporadic results, but France wanted more. There was covert professionalism at club level as teams chased success in a passionately supported domestic league. And so, in 1931, the international side found itself persona non grata as far as the international championship was concerned. There was a thaw in relations in 1939, but the outbreak of war meant that France would not return to the fold until the 1947-48 season.

In France's absence the other four nations all tasted success. Wales ended a dismal run by winning the title in 1931. The economic depression of the 1920s had hit Wales particularly hard, and Welsh rugby suffered badly as some players went north to take up the professional game. The international side won just eight out of 13 matches against the home nations during that decade. It was a different story in the 1930s, as players of the stature of Cliff Jones and Haydn Tanner emerged. The Welsh also took a share of the title in 1932 and won it outright again in 1936. In the latter year they crowned their success with an outstanding 13-12 win over Jack Manchester's All Blacks side.

Opposite: England get the ball in a line out during the England v France match of 1947, the first time France had taken part in the competition since 1931. Below: England v Wales, 1946.

Swansong season

Scotland's form dipped briefly as the great 1920s side broke up, but they did notch two Triple Crowns, in 1933 and 1938. 1933 was the swansong season for the Scots' brilliant winger Ian Smith, who helped them to their seventh Triple Crown. The eighth was claimed five years later. 1938 went down in Scottish rugby history as Wilson Shaw led the side to a 21-16 win at Twickenham. Shaw's two tries helped to seal the victory in England's back yard which they hadn't achieved for 12 years and wouldn't do again for another 33.

England themselves recorded two championship wins during this period, in 1934 and 1937. One of the stars of the side during this period was the exiled Russian prince Alexander Obolensky, who was tragically killed in a flight training accident in the early days of World War Two.

Ireland had one outright success, in 1935, their first for 36 years. The record books would have looked very different had it not been for the Welsh, who denied them the Triple Crown on four occasions during the 1930s. That included the 1939 season, the last before hostilities meant a seven-year suspension of the competition. After beating England at Twickenham and Scotland in Dublin, Irish hopes were yet again dashed with a 7-0 defeat by Wales in Belfast. Instead of outright victory, the Irish had to share the title with England and Wales.

Ireland's golden era

The immediate postwar period was one of the greatest in the country's history. Jack Kyle inspired the team to seven wins out of their eight matches in 1948 and 1949, which meant back-to-back Triple Crowns and, in the former year, the Grand Slam, Ireland's only clean sweep to date. They made it three championships in four years in 1951. Although Kyle played until 1958, success thereafter proved elusive. The Irishman found himself up against a new young Welsh star fly- half, Cliff Morgan. The two faced each other six times during the 1950s, and although Kyle may have had the better of their personal battles, he was on the winning side just once. Wales not only dominated Ireland in the 1950s, they pretty much got the better of the rest of the opposition too. They won or shared the championship five times in seven years, including Grand Slams in 1950 and 1952. As well as Morgan, the Welsh side boasted players of the quality of Bleddyn Williams, Ken Jones and Clem Thomas.

Above: Ireland's J. Robbins is beaten by an England player in a line-out at Twickenham, 1950.

Opposite: An Irish attack is broken up by the English pack five yards from the line. The post war years had been successful for the Irish but the mantle was passed to Wales who were dominant in the early 1950s.

Scotland's J. J. Hagarty tries to get away with the ball in the Calcutta Cup at Twickenham, 1953. England won the match 26-8.

England had to wait until 1953 to break the Wales-Ireland stranglehold. It was their first outright success since 1937. This was an era of some outstanding backs, including Jeff Butterfield, Dickie Jeeps and Peter Jackson. They helped England to the 1957 and 1958 championship too, the former year seeing the nation claim their first Grand Slam since 1928 and seventh all told.

French sparkle

The situation regarding French rugby was hardly different from that which had seen the country ostracised in 1931. There were further warnings by the authorities in the early 1950s, but these were not carried through. If there was an element of professionalism in French rugby, it certainly helped their performances on the pitch. They played dazzling 15-man rugby which was not only a joy to watch but which produced results. The team took a share of the spoils in 1954, losing only to Wales in Cardiff. Another share of the championship followed in 1955. After a dire season in 1957, when they lost every match, France embarked on a sparkling run of success. Lucien Mias, who had retired in in 1954, was persuaded to return and he was the architect behind a string of excellent results. A 16-6 win in Cardiff, France's first on Welsh soil, made everyone sit up and take notice, as did a victory over the mighty Springboks in South Africa, something that neither the British Lions nor the All

England v Scotland 1979. Horton gets up for England in a match that ended all square.

Blacks had managed. France followed this up with a first outright win in the championship in 1959. They shared top spot with England in 1960, then enjoyed two more outright wins in the following

Opposite: England captain Billy Beaumont leaps above the Welsh pack at Cardiff Arms Park, March 1979. Wales won by 27 points to three to clinch their fourth successive triple crown and fourth championship in five years.

two seasons. By the end of 1961 France was on an an unbeaten 18-match run, one which was only ended by a 3-0 series defeat at the hands of the All Blacks that year.

France had further successes in 1967 and 1968, with a first Grand Slam in the latter season. But these were victories for efficient rugby rather than the champagne-style of play with which they had become associated. Two of the country's greatest ever forwards, Benoit Dauga and Walter Spanghero, were teammates in the successes, although they couldn't stand the sight of each other. Jo Maso emerged as one of the most scintillating three-quarters in world rugby, although France's new style of play meant that his talents were underused.

Welsh dream team

While France retrenched into a less expansive style of play, Wales took over as the dream team. In the 15 championships between 1964 and 1979 (the 1972 series was not completed), Wales were champions eight times and shared the title on three other occasions. There were seven

Triple Crowns in this era, and Grand Slams in 1971, 1976 and 1978. The Welsh selectors had an embarrassment of riches: Gareth Edwards, Barry John, JPR Williams, J.J. Williams, Gerald Davies, Mervyn Davies, John Dawes and Phil Bennett, to name but a few. The climax to the 1976 season saw Wales face France at Cardiff Arms Park, both sides taking a hundred percent record into the match. With Wales leading 19-13 and time running out, JPR Williams put in a trademark crunching last-ditch tackle on the French winger Gourdon; Wales had their seventh Grand Slam.

Ireland broke Wales' stranglehold on the championship in 1974, the country's centennial year. Two years earlier, terrorist threats meant that the fixtures were not completed for the first time in the 20th century. 1973 provided the most dramatic result in the history of the championship. Each nation won twice and lost twice, and as this was long before points difference was introduced, the result was a quintuple tie.

England's barren years

When Bill Beaumont led England into the 1980 championship, the country had had no outright victory since 1963, and finished with the wooden spoon five times in the previous ten years. It was the nation's worst run since the turn of the century. England's 30-18 victory at Murrayfield gave them the Calcutta Cup, the championship, Triple Crown and Grand slam for the first time since 1957. The performances didn't convince everyone, but after such a poor run of form England were simply glad to get their name in the record books.

The rest of the 1980s remained barren years for England. All the other nations enjoyed success, notably France, who won three championships outright and shared three others. France had world class backs of the calibre of Serge Blanco and Philippe Sella during this period, yet under coach Jacques Fouroux the Gallic flair was stifled somewhat as the team's juggernaut pack dominated.

Ireland had the second best record in the 1980s and were the surprise package of the decade. In 1982 they were on a seven-match losing streak, yet with Ollie Campbell back in the side after a lengthy lay-off, Ireland claimed their first Triple Crown since 1949. All 21 points which beat Scotland at Lansdowne Road to seal victory came from Campbell's boot.

Ireland shared the championship with France the following year, and won it outright again in 1985, their last victory to date.

For Scotland it was a rollercoaster decade. In 1984 the country claimed its second Grand Slam and also drew with the All Blacks. They slumped to wooden spoon position the following year, then were revitalised in 1986, sharing the title with France. In 1990 they faced England at Murrayfield. As in 1925, the Calcutta Cup, championship, Triple Crown and Grand Slam were all at stake. England were expected to win and many souvenirs had been manufactured with that result in mind. The Scots had other ideas. Instead of running on to the field, David Sole marched his men out in a warrior-like fashion. It set the tone for a match of total commitment, won by the Scots 13-7.

England recovered from that shock defeat to claim Grand Slams in 1991and 1992. Results included a 24-0 win over Wales - almost unthinkable a decade earlier - but Geoff Cooke's men still came in for criticism over their style of play. Five more titles between 1995 and 2003 were more convincing and under Clive Woodward the team not only became the undisputed top Northern Hemisphere side but arguably the premier nation in world rugby.

Opposite England prepare to meet Wales at Twickenham in 1992 in a bid to achieve the Grand Slam in succesive years. Below: With Jon Humphreys hard on his heels Matt Dawson dives for a try in England's 60- 26 win over Wales in the Five Nations' competition in 1998.

FOUR NATIONS' CHAMPIONS
(LATER FIVE, THEN SIX NATIONS)

1882-83	England	1919-20	England, Scotland and Wales
1883-84	England	1920-21	England **
1884-85	not completed	1921-22	Wales
1885-86	England and Scotland	1922-23	England **
1886-87	Scotland	1923-24	England **
1887-88	not completed	1924-25	Scotland **
1888-89	not completed	1925-26	Scotland and Ireland
1889-90	England and Scotland	1926-27	Scotland and Ireland
1890-91	Scotland	1927-28	England **
1891-92	England	1928-29	Scotland
1892-93	Wales	1929-30	England
1893-94	Ireland	1930-31	Wales
1894-95	Scotland	1931-32	England, Wales and Ireland
1895-96	Ireland	1932-33	Scotland
1896-97	not completed	1933-34	England
1897-98	not completed	1934-35	Ireland
1898-99	Ireland	1935-36	Wales
1899-1900	Wales	1936-37	England
1900-01	Scotland	1937-38	Scotland
1901-02	Wales	1938-39	England, Wales and Ireland
1902-03	Scotland	1939-46	no competition
1903-04	Scotland	1946-47	Wales and England
1904-05	Wales	1947-48	Ireland **
1905-06	Ireland and Wales	1948-49	Ireland
1906-07	Scotland	1949-50	Wales**
1907-08	Wales**	1950-51	Ireland
1908-09	Wales **	1951-52	Wales **
1909-10	England	1952-53	England
1910-11	Wales **	1953-54	England, France and Wales
1911-12	England and Ireland	1954-55	Wales and France
1912-13	England **		
1913-14	England **		
1914-19	no competition		

Opposite: England v France, 1953. England won the game 11-0 and the competition outright for the first time since 1937. The following year England, France and Wales shared the top position.

1955-56	Wales
1956-57	England **
1957-58	England
1958-59	France
1959-60	France and England
1960-61	France
1961-62	France
1962-63	England
1963-64	Scotland and Wales
1964-65	Wales
1965-66	Wales
1966-67	France
1967-68	France**
1968-69	Wales
1969-70	Wales and France
1970-71	Wales **
1971-72	not completed
1972-73	quintuple tie
1973-74	Ireland
1974-75	Wales
1975-76	Wales**
1976-77	France**
1977-78	Wales**
1978-79	Wales
1979-80	England **
1980-81	France**
1981-82	Ireland
1982-83	France and Ireland
1983-84	Scotland **
1984-85	Ireland
1985-86	France and Scotland
1986-87	France**
1987-88	Wales and France
1988-89	France
1989-90	Scotland**
1990-91	England **
1991-92	England **

1992-93	France
1993-94	Wales
1994-95	England **
1995-96	England
1996-97	France**
1997-98	France**
1998-99	Scotland
1999-2000	England
2000-01	England
2001-02	France**
2002-03	England**

** indicates grand slam

Opposite: In a balletic move Lawrence Dallaglio tries to take the ball from France's Fabien Pelous during the England France clash in Paris in 1998.

Above: Despite winning the ball over Tony Diprose of England in this move, Victor Costello's Ireland lost the Five Nations' tie 17-35.

England's Jeremy Guscott fights off simultaneous tackles from Scottish players Shaun Longstaff and Gregor Townsend.

THE
CALCUTTA CUP

THE CALCUTTA CUP

he Calcutta Cup takes its name from the Calcutta Football Club, which disbanded in 1877 after just six years in existence. The team had suffered from lack of opposition, while games such as polo and tennis were found to be more suitable for the climate. When it was wound up, the club had funds of about £60. Rather than fritter it away on a party, the members decided to offer a trophy to the Rugby Football Union. It was decided that the cup, which was made from melted down silver rupees, should be awarded to the winners of the annual England-Scotland encounter. The first Calcutta Cup match took place at Raeburn Place, Edinburgh in 1879. It ended in a draw, each side scoring one goal.

The Duke of Edinburgh shakes hands with the Scottish team, at Twickenham, 1949.

ENGLAND – V – SCOTLAND

1871 - 2003

Year	Venue	Score	Year	Venue	Score
1871	Edinburgh	Scotland 1T-1G 1T	1904	Edinburgh	Scotland 3-6
1872	The Oval	England 1G 1DG 2T-1DG	1905	Richmond	Scotland 0-8
1873	Glasgow	Drew 0-0	1906	Edinburgh	England 9-3
1874	The Oval	England 1DG 1T	1907	Blackheath	Scotland 3-8
1875	Edinburgh	Drew 0-0	1908	Edinburgh	Scotland 10-16
1876	The Oval	England 1G 1T-0	1909	Richmond	Scotland 8-18
1877	Edinburgh	Scotland 0-1DG	1910	Edinburgh	England 14-5
1878	The Oval	Drew 0-0	1911	Twickenham	England 13-8
1879	Edinburgh	Drew 1G-1DG	1912	Edinburgh	Scotland 3-8
1880	Manchester	England 2G 3T-1G	1913	Twickenham	England 3-0
1881	Edinburgh	Drew 1DG 1T-1G 1T	1914	Edinburgh	England 16-15
1882	Manchester	Scotland 0-2T	1920	Twickenham	England 13-4
1883	Edinburgh	England 2T-1T	1921	Edinburgh	England 18-0
1884	Blackheath	England 1G-1T	1922	Twickenham	England 11-5
1886	Edinburgh	Drew 0-0	1923	Edinburgh	England 8-6
1887	Manchester	Drew 1T-1T	1924	Twickenham	England 19-0
1890	Edinburgh	England 1G-1T-0	1925	Edinburgh	Scotland 11-14
1891	Richmond	Scotland 3-9	1926	Twickenham	Scotland 9-17
1892	Edinburgh	England 5-0	1927	Edinburgh	Scotland 13-21
1893	Leeds	Scotland 0-8	1928	Twickenham	England 6-0
1894	Edinburgh	Scotland 0-6	1929	Edinburgh	Scotland 6-12
1895	Richmond	Scotland 3-6	1930	Twickenham	Drew 0-0
1896	Glasgow	Scotland 0-11	1931	Edinburgh	Scotland 19-28
1897	Manchester	England 12-3	1932	Twickenham	England 16-3
1898	Edinburgh	Drew 3-3	1933	Edinburgh	Scotland 0-3
1899	Blackheath	Scotland 0-5	1934	Twickenham	England 6-3
1900	Edinburg	Drew 0-0	1935	Edinburgh	Scotland 7-10
1901	Blackheath	Scotland 3-18	1936	Twickenham	England 9-8
1902	Edinburgh	England 6-3	1937	Edinburgh	England 6-3
1903	Richmond	Scotland 6-10	1938	Twickenham	Scotland 16-21

Year	Venue	Score	Year	Venue	Score
1939	Edinburgh	England 9-6	1960	Edinburgh	England 21-12
1947	Twickenham	England 24-5	1961	Twickenham	England 6-0
1948	Edinburgh	Scotland 3-6	1962	Edinburgh	Drew 3-3
1949	Twickenham	England 19-3	1963	Twickenham	England 10-8
1950	Edinburgh	Scotland 11-13	1964	Edinburgh	Scotland 6-15
1951	Twickenham	England 5-3	1965	Twickenham	Drew 3-3
1952	Edinburgh	England 19-3	1966	Edinburgh	Scotland 3-6
1953	Twickenham	England 26-8	1967	Twickenham	England 27-14
1954	Edinburgh	England 13-3	1968	Edinburgh	England 8-6
1955	Twickenham	England 9-6	1969	Twickenham	England 8-3
1956	Edinburgh	England 11-6	1970	Edinburgh	Scotland 5-14
1957	Twickenham	England 16-3	1971	Twickenham	Scotland 15-16
1958	Edinburgh	Drew 3-3	1971	Edinburgh	Scotland 6-26
1959	Twickenham	Drew 3-3	1972	Edinburgh	Scotland 9-23

Year	Venue	Score	Year	Venue	Score
1973	Twickenham	England 20-13	1989	Twickenham	Drew 12-12
1974	Edinburgh	Scotland 14-16	1990	Edinburgh	Scotland 7-13
1975	Twickenham	England 7-6	1991	Twickenham	England 21-12
1976	Edinburgh	Scotland 12-22	1991	Edinburgh	England 9-6
1977	Twickenham	England 26-6	1992	Edinburgh	England 25-7
1978	Edinburgh	England 15-0	1993	Twickenham	England 26-12
1979	Twickenham	Drew 7-7	1994	Edinburgh	England 15-14
1980	Edinburgh	England 30-18	1995	Twickenham	England 24-12
1981	Twickenham	England 23-17	1996	Edinburgh	England 18-9
1982	Edinburgh	Drew 9-9	1997	Twickenham	England 41-13
1983	Twickenham	Scotland 12-22	1998	Edinburgh	England 34-20
1984	Edinburgh	Scotland 6-18	1999	Twickenham	England 24-21
1985	Twickenham	England 10-7	2000	Edinburgh	Scotland 13-19
1986	Edinburgh	Scotland 6-33	2001	Twickenham	England 43-3
1987	Twickenham	England 21-12	2002	Edinburgh	England 29-3
1988	Edinburgh	England 9-6	2003	Twickenham	England 40-9

Above right: England's J.E. Williams passes out from a scrum in the 1955 tie. England won 9-6.
Above left : Gavin Hastings (left) and Will Carling, rivals in the Calcutta Cup, pictured
together during a Lions training session at the Stoop in 1993.
Opposite: Players jump during a line out in an England v Scotland match
at Twickenham in 1975. England won the match 7-6.

THE RUGBY
WORLD CUP

The natural conservatism of the IRB meant that rugby was just about the last major sport to embrace the idea of a world cup. In the early 1980s Australia and New Zealand made representations to the game's administrators. With South Africa in the sporting wilderness, these were the two dominant rugby-playing nations and were no doubt keen on the idea of staging a tournament they would be favourites to win. The Five Nations countries were less enthusiastic, perhaps feeling that such a competition would undermine their own. Another factor was the possibility of a rebel professional tour, along the lines of Kerry Packer's cricket circus of the previous decade. This no doubt concentrated the minds of the officials, who wanted to run the show if it was going to take place at all.

Agreement was finally reached in 1985, with South Africa voting in favour despite the fact that it would be unable to compete. The Springboks were excluded for political reasons, a decision the country itself endorsed. 1986 was considered too soon, 1988 was Olympic year, so 1987 was settled upon for the inaugural tournament.

Opposite: England v Australia in the 1991 World Cup final at Twickenham Australia won by 12 points to 6

1987 WORLD CUP

Australia and New Zealand

t was staged in Australia and New Zealand. Sixteen countries were represented, and entry was by invitation only; there were no qualifying matches. After all the big guns were pencilled in - minus South Africa - the IRB opted for a geographical spread to give the event a global flavour. That made for some anomalies, for example the inclusion of the USA while Western Samoa were left out in the cold.

The lack of depth at the highest level meant that many of the group matches was somewhat academic. New Zealand opened their account with a record 70-6 win over Italy. It also provided the try of the tournament as All Blacks' winger John Kirwan ran in a length-of-the-field try.

The only seeding hiccup en-route to the quarter-finals came in Pool Three, where Argentina surprisingly went down to Fiji and were relegated to third spot. The Fijians had been guilty of a cynical tactical ploy, resting several of their players for the New Zealand match, which they knew they couldn't win. Scotland drew with France and looked the strongest of the British contingent, despite the fact that Wales completed their group matches with maximum points.

The Scots finished second to France on countback and had to face New Zealand in the last eight. They had no answer, going down 30-3. Fiji made a spirited fight of their match with France and went out with heads held high. The Australians booked their semi-final berth with victory over Ireland to ensure that the "big three" were all in the shake-up. Wales were the surprise package. It was almost a decade since they'd won the Five Nations, but put England out to reach the last four.

The New Zealand juggernaut rolled on in the semis, their 49-6 win over Wales being the biggest margin ever between those two countries. The other match was a thrilling encounter at Concord Oval, Sydney. France snatched victory, Serge Blanco's late try in the corner ending Australia's hopes. The Australians were so devastated that they also succumbed to Wales in the play-off. They took no pleasure in picking up fourth-place medals.

Unfortunately, the French couldn't reproduce their best form in the showpiece final, staged at Auckland's Eden Park stadium. It wasn't a match worthy of the occasion, but the All Blacks racked up another 29 points to be crowned world champions. They had scored 298 points in the six matches, Grant Fox alone bagging 126 of them. David Kirk thus became the first man to lift the William Webb Ellis

Trophy, although some ruefully commented that with so few genuine contenders for top spot, a World Cup without the Springboks was badly weakened.

The tournament hadn't had many exciting matches, but it was up and running. The four-yearly cycle was soon confirmed and all eyes were now on 1991, when Britain, Ireland and France would host the event.

WORLD CUP RESULTS 1987

POOL ONE

Australia	19 - 6	England
USA	21 - 18	Japan
England	60 - 7	Japan
Australia	47 - 12	USA
England	34 - 6	USA
Australia	42 - 23	Japan

	P	W	D	L	F	A	PTS
Australia	3	3	0	0	108	41	6
England	3	2	0	1	100	32	4
USA	3	1	0	2	39	99	2
Japan	3	0	0	3	48	123	0

POOL TWO

Canada	37 - 4	Tonga
Wales	13 - 6	Ireland
Wales	29 - 16	Tonga
Ireland	46 - 19	Canada
Wales	40 - 9	Canada
Ireland	32 - 9	Tonga

	P	W	D	L	F	A	PTS
Wales	3	3	0	0	82	31	6
Ireland	3	2	0	1	84	41	4
Canada	3	1	0	2	65	90	2
Tonga	3	0	0	3	29	98	0

POOL THREE

New Zealand	70 - 6	Italy
Fiji	28 -9	Argentina
New Zealand	74 - 13	Fiji
Argentina	25 - 16	Italy
Italy	18 - 15	Fiji
New Zealand	46 - 15	Argentina

	P	W	D	L	F	A	PTS
New Zealand	3	3	0	0	190	34	6
Fiji	3	1	0	2	56	101	2
Argentina	3	1	0	2	49	90	2
Italy	3	1	0	2	40	110	2

POOL FOUR

Romania	21 - 20	Zimbabwe
France	20 - 20	Scotland
France	55 - 12	Romania
Scotland	60 - 21	Zimbabwe
Scotland	55 - 28	Romania
France	70 - 12	Zimbabwe

	P	W	D	L	F	A	PTS
France	3	2	1	0	145	44	5
Scotland	3	2	1	0	135	69	5
Romania	3	1	0	2	61	130	2
Zimbabwe	3	0	0	3	53	151	0

QUARTER-FINALS

New Zealand 30 - 3 Scotland   France 31 - 16 Fiji
Australia 33 - 15 Ireland   Wales 16 - 3 England

SEMI-FINALS

France 30 - 24 Australia   New Zealand 49 - 6 Wales

THIRD PLACE PLAY-OFF   **FINAL**
Wales 22 - 21 Australia.   New Zealand 29 - 9 France

1991 WORLD CUP
Britain, Ireland and France

s in 1987, sixteen teams contested the 1991 World Cup, which was staged in Britain, Ireland and France. The top eight teams from the inaugural tournament were there as of right, with the remaining places decided by a qualification series. The pool matches were notable for two upsets, Canada and Western Samoa reaching the quarter-finals at the expense of Fiji and Wales respectively. Wales 16-13 defeat by Western Samoa represented a new low point in that country's fortunes, while the Pacific Islanders proved it was no fluke with a comfortable victory over Argentina.

Holders New Zealand qualified comfortably, then eased their way into the semis with a victory over Canada. The quarter-final between Australia and Ireland was the match of the tournament. With a couple of minutes to go Ireland held a three-point advantage. Their dream was then shattered by Michael Lynagh. For once it wasn't the Australian fly-half's golden boot that did the damage. Lynagh's kicking game had gone noticeably off the boil, but here it was his coolness under pressure that won the day. After Ireland scored he told his men he would kick off deep, and that if the forwards could win the ball and feed the back line, they would score. It worked out perfectly, Lynagh himself touching down for the score which put Australia into the semi-finals by a single point.

England reach the Final

Having put out France in the last eight, England reached the final with a narrow 9-6 win over Scotland. At two penalties apiece, Rob Andrew dropped the all-important goal which secured victory. It was the 15th of his international career, equaling the world record. It left Gavin Hastings rueing a late missed penalty which was a simple opportunity by his high standards. England were through, but it was hardly scintillating rugby.

By contrast, Australia's 16-6 win over the holders was a pulsating affair. David Campese scored after seven minutes, and after a Lynagh penalty, Tim Horan also went over to give the Australians a 13-0 lead at half-time. The All Blacks had to play catch-up and had enough possession to do so, but Australia's defence was immense. They swarmed all over the All Blacks, and if the first tackler was unsuccessful, there was always a second on hand. At the end they had just two Grant Fox goals to show for their afternoon's work, and it is doubtful whether Michael Jones - their superb

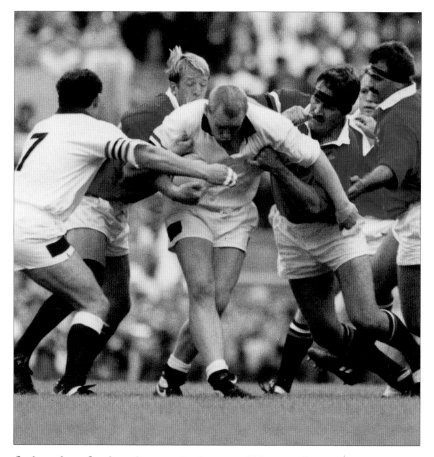

flanker who refused to play on a Sunday - would have made any difference to the outcome.

Above: England defeat the USA by 37 points to 9.

England surprised everyone by playing more expansively in the final, prompting former All Blacks captain David Kirk to comment that this was hardly the time to practise passing! Geoff Cooke's men never looked likely to breach the resilient Australian defence, however, and were restricted to two second-half penalties. Australia scored the only try of the match, prop forward Daly going over from a drive following a line-out. Coach Bob Dwyer praised his side's defence after their 12-6 victory. The Wallabies had conceded just three tries during the tournament, two of those against Argentina, and were worthy winners.

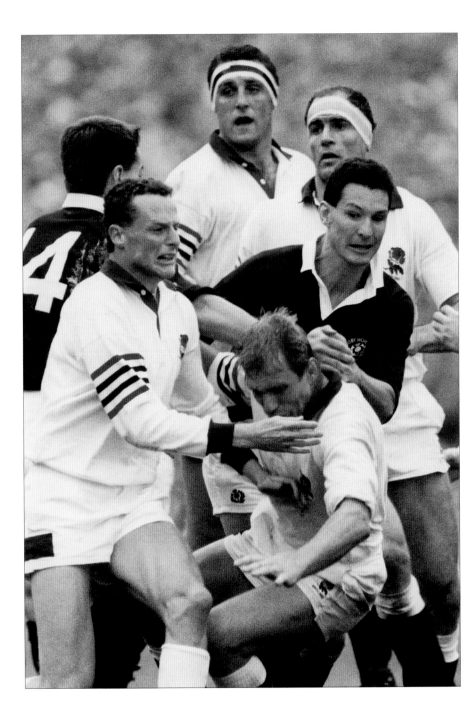

WORLD CUP RESULTS 1991

(Teams awarded 3 points for a win, 2 points for a draw and,
if defeated, 1 point for fulfilling the fixture)

POOL ONE

England	12-18	New Zealand
Italy	30-9	United States
New Zealand	46-6	United States
England	36-6	Italy
England	37-9	United States
New Zealand	31-21	Italy

	P	W	D	L	F	A	PTS
New Zealand	3	3	0	0	95	39	9
England	3	2	0	1	85	33	7
Italy	3	1	0	2	57	76	5
USA	3	0	0	3	24	113	3

POOL TWO

Scotland	47-9	Japan
Ireland	55-11	Zimbabwe
Ireland	32-16	Japan
Scotland	51-12	Zimbabwe
Scotland	24-15	Ireland
Zimbabwe	8-52	Japan

	P	W	D	L	F	A	PTS
Scotland	3	3	0	0	122	36	9
Ireland	3	2	0	1	102	51	7
Japan	3	1	0	2	77	87	5
Zimbabwe	3	0	0	3	31	158	3

POOL THREE

Australian	32-19	Argentina
Wales	13-16	Western Samoa
Australia	9-3	Western Samoa
Wales	16-7	Argentina
Wales	3-38	Australia
Argentina	12-35	Western Samoa

	P	W	D	L	F	A	PTS
Australia	3	3	0	0	79	25	9
W Samoa	3	2	0	1	54	34	7
Wales	3	1	0	2	32	61	5
Argentina	3	0	0	3	38	83	3

POOL FOUR

France	30-3	Romania
Fiji	3-13	Canada
France	33-9	Fiji
Canada	19-11	Romania
Romania	17-15	Fiji
France	19-13	Canada

	P	W	D	L	F	A	PTS
France	3	3	0	0	82	25	9
Canada	3	2	0	1	45	33	7
Romania	3	1	0	2	31	64	5
Fiji	3	0	0	3	27	63	3

QUARTERFINALS

Scotland 28 - 6 Western Samoa   France 10-19 England

Australia 19-18 Ireland   New Zealand 29-13 Canada

SEMI-FINALS

Scotland 6-9 England   Australia 16-6 New Zealand

THIRD PLACE PLAY-OFF

New Zealand 13-6 Scotland

*Opposite: Scotland v England
in the semi-final of the 1991
Rugby World Cup which
England won by 9 points to 6.*

Final

Australia 12 -6 England

1995 WORLD CUP
South Africa

A 1995 saw the Rainbow Nation admitted to the international fold. South Africa celebrated its return by hosting the tournament and promptly began to show that years of isolation had done nothing to dent its sporting edge.

As in 1991, the top eight teams from the previous tournament took their places automatically. This time, however, as the hosts were not among those quarter-finalists, just seven places were up for grabs in the qualification series.

The opening fixture saw a clash of two giants as South Africa took on holders Australia. South Africa ran out 27-18 winners, but both of Pool A's big guns eased into the knockout stage.

Lomu sensation

New Zealand posted their intention to recapture their crown by racking up 225 points in their three group matches, including a record 145-17 demolition of Japan. Fly-half Andrew Mehrtens was in excellent form, and would go on to finish the tournament with an aggregate of 31 successful kicks - including three drop goals - plus a try. But the sensation was his teammate, 19-year-old Jonah Lomu. 35 points from seven tries meant that the giant left-wing just scraped into the top ten highest scorers, but all of those above him in the list were specialists with the boot.

England and France looked like providing the main threat from the northern hemisphere teams, and both reached the last eight without dropping a point. There was a tragedy in the final match of Pool D, when the Ivory Coast's Max Brito was paralysed in a match against Tonga, a game in which there was nothing at stake but the group's minor placings.

England lose semi-final to the All Blacks

The tie of the quarter-finals was the England-Australia clash, a repeat of the final four years earlier. The scores were tied at 22-22 deep into injury-time, when England scrum-half Dewi Morris fed Rob Andrew, who sent over a monster drop goal to clinch a famous victory over the holders. That set up a semi-final encounter against the All Blacks, who put out Scotland 48-30.

The New Zealand-England clash was virtually a one-man show. Time and again Jonah Lomu bulldozed his way through England's defence. England's Tony Underwood had no chance of containing his opposite number. Bigger men tried to stop Lomu, and they too either bounced off him or were swatted aside. After the 45-29 defeat, which included four Lomu tries, England captain Will Carling unsurprisingly said that one man was the difference between the two sides.

France and South Africa contested the other semi, which was a much closer affair. The home side squeezed through on a waterlogged Durban pitch, but the French were left wringing their hands over a disallowed try which they believed should have stood. Christophe Deylaud had not been in good form at fly-half, and Frank Mesnel was handed the No 10 shirt for the 3rd-4th place playoff, in which France beat England 19-9.

South Africa victorious

The final was no try-fest, but it was gripping stuff all the same. New Zealand enjoyed a lot of possession but couldn't turn it into points on the board as the Springbok defence held firm. It was a fascinating match in which the All Blacks tried to stretch the play, while South Africa countered by keeping it narrow and plugging all the gaps. The Springboks led 9-6 at half-time. An Andrew Mehrtens drop goal levelled the score midway through the second period, and the game went into extra-time. Mehrtens put New Zealand 12-9 ahead with a penalty, but

it was to be his opposite number, Joel Stransky, who was to be the the hero of the hour. Stransky had been an unheralded member of the South Africa side, and in the run-up to the tournament was not even assured of a place in the starting line-up. But over the five weeks he became the star of the show. He levelled the score with a penalty, then, with seven minutes left, floated over a glorious 30-metre drop goal which won the match. Ellis Park went wild as President Nelson Mandela, wearing a replica shirt, awarded South Africa captain Francois Pienaar the trophy.

With a red Welsh dragon painted on his face, this youngster is engrossed in the Rugby World Cup.

Above: French winger, Ntamack, fights off South African players during the rain-soaked semi-final at King's Park stadium.

WORLD CUP RESULTS 1995

POOL A

South Africa	27 -18	Australia
Canada	34 - 3	Romania
South Africa	21 - 8	Romania
Australia	27 - 11	Canada
Australia	42 - 3	Romania
South Africa	20 - 0	Canada

	P	W	D	L	F	A	PTS
South Africa	3	3	0	0	68	26	9
Australia	3	2	0	1	87	41	7
Canada	3	1	0	2	45	50	5
Romania	3	0	0	3	14	97	3

POOL B

W Samoa	43 - 18	Italy
England	24 - 18	Argentina
W Samoa	32 - 26	Argentina
England	27 - 20	Italy
Italy	31 - 25	Argentina
England	44 - 22	W Samoa

	P	W	D	L	F	A	PTS
England	3	3	0	0	95	60	9
W Samoa	3	2	0	1	96	88	7
Italy	3	1	0	2	69	94	5
Argentina	3	0	0	3	69	87	3

POOL C

Wales	57 - 10	Japan
New Zealand	43 - 19	Ireland
Ireland	50 - 28	Japan
New Zealand	34 - 9	Wales
New Zealand	145 - 17	Japan
Ireland	24 - 23	Wales

	P	W	D	L	F	A	PTS
New Zealand	3	3	0	0	222	45	9
Ireland	3	2	0	1	93	94	7
Wales	3	1	0	2	89	68	5
Japan	3	0	0	3	47	252	3

POOL D

Scotland	89 - 0	Ivory Coast
France	38 - 10	Tonga
France	54 - 18	Ivory Coast
Scotland	41 - 5	Tonga
Tonga	29 - 11	Ivory Coast
France	22 - 19	Scotland

	P	W	D	L	F	A	PTS
France	3	3	0	0	114	47	9
Scotland	3	2	0	1	147	27	7
Tonga	3	1	0	2	44	90	5
Ivory Coast	3	0	0	3	29	172	3

QUARTER-FINALS

France 36 - 12 Ireland   South Africa 42 - 14 Western Samoa

England 25 - 22 Australia   New Zealand 48 - 30 Scotland

SEMI-FINALS

France 15 - 19 South Africa   New Zealand 45 - 29 England

THIRD PLACE PLAY-OFF

France 19 - 9 England

FINAL

South Africa 15 - 12 New Zealand

1999 WORLD CUP

Wales

T he 1999 tournament was nominally staged in Wales, although for political purposes all the other Five Nations countries hosted matches too. It was also an expanded 20-team competition. Only the top three finishers from 1995 - South Africa, New Zealand and France - together with hosts Wales, qualified automatically. This left 66 countries scrambling for the the remaining 16 places.

Five pools meant that a repechage system was implemented, with only the group winners guaranteed a quarter-final place.

In Pool A South Africa ran out 46-29 winners over Scotland in the deciding match, after both had beaten World Cup debutants Spain and Uruguay. The Scots had led the Springboks 19-18 when they lost their Kiwi-born centre John Leslie. They conceded four late tries and had to be content with a place in the play-offs.

England and New Zealand both hit a ton in Pool B, against Tonga and Italy respectively. The two big guns had already met by then. Mehrtens and Wilkinson kicked three penalties each, but the New Zealander also had three tries to convert, Wilkinson only one.

Fijians scare French

France came into the tournament on a poor run of form, but with legends Pierre Villepreux and Jean-Claude Skrela at the helm they came good at last. Not without a scare, however, particularly in the final group match against Fiji. The Pacific islanders led 19-13 at one stage, and were also denied seven vital points when a try was disallowed. The French took the lead with a penalty try after a succession of set scrums near the Fijian line, and sealed victory when Christophe Dominici went over.

Graham Henry's Wales side took top spot in Pool D, despite a 38-31 reversal at the hands of Western Samoa. It set up a quarter-final clash with Australia, but Wales showed nothing like the form which had seen them go on a 10-match unbeaten run over the previous year. Argentina's victory over Western Samoa assured them of a place in the play-offs as the best third-placed team.

Australia won Pool E, without ever looking totally convincing. They conceded a try against the USA, and their 23-3 win over Ireland, the key group fixture, was a dull affair.

Argentina were the surprise package of the tournament, beating Ireland 28-24 in the play-offs. The Irish held a 15-9 advantage at half-time, all their points courtesy

4:38 New Zealand 31 France 43

of Humphreys' boot. But an Albanese try, converted by Gonzalo Quesada, changed everything, and Argentina's defence held firm to secure a famous victory. Scotland and England successfully negotiated their second-round matches, beating Samoa and Fiji respectively.

The quarter-finals saw the three remaining home nations crash out, all to southern hemisphere opposition. It meant that for the first time in World Cup history there would be no United Kingdom representation at the semi-final stage. Two tries from Tana Umaga and one from Jeff Wilson left Scotland playing catch-up against New Zealand at Murrayfield. The Scots actually won the second

French players wave the Tricolour in celebration of their defeat of New Zealand in the semi-final of the 1999 World Cup.

half battle, but a try from Lomu proved that there was only ever going to be one winner.

England's hopes were dashed by the boot of South Africa's Jannie de Beer. A world record five drop goals did most of the damage, with five penalties and two conversions piling on the agony for England.

Neil Jenkins' record points score

Wales had just three Neil Jenkins penalties to show for their efforts against Australia. As half-time approached the Welsh trailed just 10-9, but when Ben Tune pounced onto a Steve Larkham chip the gap was suddenly eight points. Scrum half George Gregan went over twice to book Australia's place in the last four. The Welsh complained that one of those came after a forward pass, but they had hardly done enough to justify a semi-final berth. For Jenkins there was the consolation of becoming the highest points scorer in test rugby, having passed Michael Lynagh's mark of 892 in the match against Western Samoa. Jenkins' 9 points against the Wallabies put him on 927.

The tie of the round was France's thrilling 47-26 win over Argentina in Dublin. The French ran in five tries to Argentina's two. Gonzalo Quesada converted both of his team's scores and also struck three penalties to put him on 102 points, which would make him the tournament's top scorer.

Below: Australia's George Gregan gets the ball out at an exciting moment in Australia's 35-12 win over France in the Final of the 1999 World Cup

The French followed this up by contesting the match of the tournament with New Zealand. They had gone down by 50 points in their previous meeting with the All Blacks, but this time it was a glorious victory for Villepreux's men. Christophe Lamaison scored a marvellous try for France, but Lomu crossed the line twice to help New Zealand take a 24-10 lead early in the second half. Two penalties and two drop goals from Lamaison brought France back into contention. Three converted tries then followed to leave the All Blacks totally stunned. The French had scored 33 points without reply, and a late Jeff Wilson try was but a consolation.

Australia make the Final again

The Australia-South Africa semi had no tries but was also full of drama. Jannie de Beer levelled the scores with a penalty that was also the last kick of the match. But it was to no avail as a Larkham drop goal and Matt Burke penalty in extra-time put Australia into the final for the second time.

The 3rd-4th place play-off was thus a repeat of the 1995 final. South Africa came out on top yet again, New Zealand still reeling from that semi-final defeat. All Blacks coach John Hart would soon pay the price of failure.

The final was not a great game. The French could not reproduce the form of the previous two rounds and were contained brilliantly by Australia's defence. Their 12 points came from four Lamaison penalties, and as they ran out of steam they conceded two late tries to make the final margin of Australia's victory comfortable. Having gone into the tournament as Five Nations wooden spoonists, the French side had acquitted itself superbly and returned home to a rapturous reception. But it was the Wallabies' day. John Eales lifted the trophy as Australia celebrated becoming the first country to win the tournament twice.

WORLD CUP RESULTS 1999

Pool A

Spain	15-27	Uruguay
Scotland	29-46	South Africa
Scotland	43-12	Uruguay
South Africa	47-3	Spain
South Africa	39-3	Uruguay
Scotland	48-0	Spain

	P	W	D	L	F	A	PTS
South Africa	3	3	0	0	132	35	9
Scotland	3	2	0	1	120	58	7
Uruguay	3	1	0	2	42	97	5
Spain	3	0	0	3	18	122	3

Pool B

England	67-7	Italy
New Zealand	45-9	Tonga
England	16-30	New Zealand
Italy	25-28	Tonga
New Zealand	101-3	Italy
England	101-10	Tonga

	P	W	D	L	F	A	PTS
New Zealand	3	3	0	0	176	28	9
England	3	2	0	1	184	47	7
Tonga	3	1	0	2	47	171	5
Italy	3	0	0	3	35	196	3

Pool C

Fiji	67-18	Namibia
France	33-20	Canada
France	47-13	Namibia
Fiji	38-22	Canada
Canada	72-11	Namibia
France	28-19	Fiji

	P	W	D	L	F	A	PTS
France	3	3	0	0	108	52	9
Fiji	3	2	0	1	124	68	7
Canada	3	1	0	2	114	82	5
Namibia	3	0	0	3	42	186	3

Pool D

Wales	23-18	Argentina
W Samoa	43-9	Japan
Wales	64-15	Japan
Argentina	32-16	W Samoa
Wales	31-38	W Samoa
Argentina	33-12	Japan

	P	W	D	L	F	A	PTS
Wales	3	2	0	1	118	71	7
W Samoa	3	2	0	1	97	72	7
Argentina	3	2	0	1	83	51	7
Japan	3	0	0	3	36	140	3

Pool E

Ireland	53-8	USA
Australia	57-9	Romania
USA	25-27	Romania
Ireland	3-23	Australia
Australia	55-19	USA
Ireland	44-14	Romania

	P	W	D	L	F	A	PTS
Australia	3	3	0	0	135	31	9
Ireland	3	2	0	1	100	45	7
Romania	3	1	0	2	50	126	5
USA	3	0	0	3	52	135	3

Play-off matches

Ireland	24-28	Argentina
Scotland	35-20	Western Samoa
England	45-24	Fiji

Quarter-finals

Wales	9-24	Australia
New Zealand	30-18	Scotland
France	47-26	Argentina
South Africa	44-21	England

Semi-finals

Australia 27-21 South Africa
(a.e.t. 18-18 after 80 minutes)

France 43-31 New Zealand

3rd-4th place play-off

South Africa 22-18 New Zealand

Final

Australia 35-12 France

Australia on their way to victory against France in the Final of the 1999 World Cup (above) and (below) celebrating with the Webb Ellis trophy.

THE RUGBY WORLD CUP 2003

The 2003 tournament will be staged in Australia, beginning on 10 October and culminating on 22 November, when the final will be held at Sydney's Stadium Australia.

The International Rugby Board decided to change the qualification rules yet again. As in 1991 and 1995, all eight quarter-finalists from the preceding tournament were awarded automatic qualification. This meant that Australia, France, South Africa, New Zealand, England, Scotland, Wales and Argentina didn't have to scrap it out in the exhaustive round of zonal matches to secure their places. 82 other countries did, battling for the remaining 12 places that were up for grabs. Ten of those were filled as follows:

AFRICA	AMERICAS	ASIA	EUROPE	OCEANIA
Namibia	Canada	Japan	Ireland	Fiji
	Uruguay		Italy	Samoa
			Romania	
			Georgia	

The countries from each zone which just missed out on qualification went into a repechage round, which was used to fill the remaining two places. Tonga and the USA won through from this series.

Unlike 1999, the 20 competing teams will be put into four pools of five. After the round-robin matches, the top two teams in each group will go forward into the quarter-finals; there will be no play-off matches.

POOL A	POOL B	POOL C	POOL D
Australia	France	South Africa	New Zealand
Argentina	Scotland	England	Wales
Ireland	Fiji	Samoa	Canada
Romania	Japan	Uruguay	Italy
Namibia	USA	Georgia	Tonga

Opposite: Jonny Wilkinson celebrates after scoring a try in England's massive victory, 67-7, over Italy in the 1999 World Cup.

WORLD CUP FACTFILE

TOP TRY SCORERS:

1 Jonah Lomu   15
2 Rory Underwood   11
3 David Campese   10

TOP TRY SCORERS IN EACH TOURNAMENT:

1987   Craig Green and John Kirwan (both New Zealand) each scored 6

1991   David Campese (Australia) and Jean-Baptiste Lafond (France) each scored 6

1995   Jonah Lomu and Marc Ellis (both New Zealand) each scored 7

1999   Jonah Lomu (New Zealand) scored 8

MOST TRIES IN A MATCH:

6, by Marc Ellis for New Zealand against Japan in 1995

TOP POINTS SCORERS IN EACH TOURNAMENT:

1987   Grant Fox (New Zealand) 126
1991   Ralph Keyes (Ireland) 68
1995   Thierry Lacroix (France) 112
1999   Gonzdalo Quesada (Argentina) 102

MOST POINTS IN A MATCH:

45, by Simon Culhane for New Zealand against Japan in 1995

MOST WINS:

New Zealand - 20

MOST DEFEATS:

Japan - 11

BIGGEST MARGIN OF VICTORY:

New Zealand 145 Japan 17 (1995)

TOP POINTS SCORERS

	TRIES	CONVERSIONS	PENS	DROP GOALS	TOTAL
1 Gavin Hastings (Scotland)	9	39	36	0	227
2 Michael Lynagh (Australia)	4	36	33	2	195
3 Grant Fox (New Zealand)	0	37	31	1	170

Canada's Gareth Rees is the only player to have appeared in all four World Cups to date

Opposite: Will Greenwood covers for Jonny Wilkinson during a Six Nations' match against Ireland.

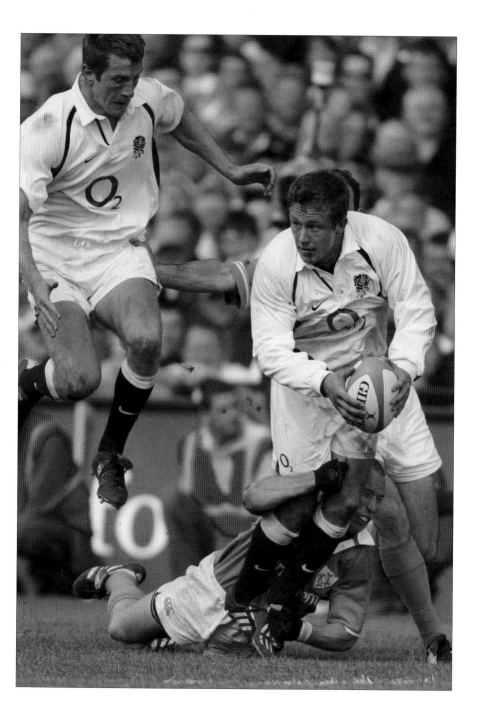

ACKNOWLEDGEMENTS

The photographs in this book are from the archives of the *Daily Mail*.
Particular thanks to
Steve Torrington, Dave Sheppard, Brian Jackson,
Alan Pinnock, Richard Jones and all the staff.

Thanks also to
Cliff Salter, Maureen Hill,
Liz Balmer, Jim Carpenter, Carol Salter, Murray Mahon,
Peter Wright, Trevor Bunting and Mark Aris.
Design by John Dunne.